Sport

Colin McGinn

ACUMEN

First published in 2008 by Acumen

Acumen Publishing Limited
Stocksfield Hall
Stocksfield
NE43 7TN
www.acumenpublishing.co.uk

ISBN: 978-1-84465-148-1

British Library Cataloguing-in-Publication Data
A catalogue record for this book is available
from the British Library.

Designed and typeset by Kate Williams, Swansea.
Printed and bound by Biddles Ltd, King's Lynn.

Contents

Preface

Sport has been important in my life, but I never thought I would write a book about it. Sport and writing were separate spheres of activity, the one in contrast to the other. But when I was asked to contribute to *The Art of Living* series, sport was the topic that most took my fancy: now I could bring the two spheres together. This required a new kind of writing from me: more about bodies than minds.

The book takes the form of a memoir, from childhood to the present (in this it resembles my intellectual memoir *The Making of a Philosopher*). This struck me as the best way to present sport as it is experienced from the inside, as a participant. It also enables me to bring out the concrete aspects of particular sports, their structure and demands. I am not dealing with sport as a detached sociologist or "cultural theorist", but as a philosophically minded practitioner. Accordingly, there is little here about the social and economic aspects of professional sports; my focus is on sport as part of the good life of an individual – as something anybody can engage in. I am interested in the value of sport as a human activity. And I am advocating it as an essential part of living well.

I have lived in America for the past twenty years, and much of my narrative relates to this phase of my life. However, I have also included my earlier British sporting years as well. The result is distinctly transatlantic, and I have been aware that my readers are likely to be from one place or the other, with different sporting cultures. I have simply straddled the continents, not attempting any false unity. Sport is perhaps more global now than ever, and this book is likewise inclusive.

Usually in the preface to a book one thanks one's intellectual colleagues for their comments and assistance. In the case of this book, I have no such obligation, since the athletic part of my life has been largely independent of the academic part. Instead I must thank some of the many people I have interacted with in an athletic context: Andrew, Keith, Bruno, Danny, John, the Martin family, Cathy, Clayton, Tony, Jim, Miguel, Greg, George, Claudio, and especially David. You taught me a lot, and not just athletically.

Colin McGinn
Miami Beach

1. From pinball to pole vault

Two early experiences of sport are burned indelibly into my memory. In one, I am at school – infant school in Gillingham, Kent, *circa* 1955 – and I am pulling myself along a horizontal beam while suspended underneath it from my arms and legs. I was about five years old and this was the first time I had held my own weight like that. I felt the pull of gravity on my small body, about three feet above the ground; a fall, although not disastrous, would have been distinctly unfortunate. There was risk, but also the sense that I could control it. As I shinned along the beam in this inverted position, aiming for the opposite end, the teacher exclaimed to the other children, "Look at Colin, he's like a monkey!" I remember feeling flattered, but also slightly miffed: she was clearly impressed with my agility (and strength!), but the feat was also deemed not quite the proper thing to do. Did she think I was "showing off"? That would never do, showing off being a mortal sin in English society. To be thought to be showing off was mortifying, blush-inducing, and really not true ... but then maybe a little, at least once I had been noticed. But primarily, it was gratifying to be compared thus to a monkey: have you seen how well they climb? Nobody joined me under the beam, however: lack of talent, I surmised.

The other experience was simpler, more elemental. I'm at the same school, maybe even younger, and it's a warm summer day. I run into the playground at full tilt, the little legs a blur – such speed! Ahead of me is a grass verge, leading up to the sports field, at an incline of about thirty degrees. As I reach it, at my maximum

1

velocity, I feel the momentum carry me effortlessly up the hill, losing speed but gaining height, and at the summit I lose all acceleration and come to a calm halt. It was the feeling of a body in motion, self-propelled, under physical forces, but controlling the movement, using the forces, to take me to a place I wanted to reach, then attaining the goal as the momentum spent itself. The moving human body, the obliging yet resistant world, the timing: all the elements of sport are there. Also the sense of autonomy, of the embodied will: a pleasant existential aloneness – muscular solipsism, as it were. Here I am, a singular being, with my own force and will, a directed agent (only a few years earlier virtually immobile in a cot).

Like many another child, my early years were spent in physical activity, as I discovered more about what the body can do. I acquired skills, played games, competed, lost and won, fell and got up, persisted, gave up, tried and tried again: not much thinking, but a lot of doing. At school I mainly played marbles, conkers (a game played by battling with horse chestnuts on strings) and what we called "faggies". In those distant days, packets of cigarettes contained small rectangular cards, known colloquially as "fag cards", which could be completed into full sets: say, British Wild Flowers or Steam Trains or Military Uniforms (as if people needed an extra incentive to smoke). They had coloured pictures on the front and some educational text on the back, and were suitable for collecting, like stamps. No doubt they had their own special artists and writers. But there was something far more impressive you could do with these cards than merely collect them: you could *flick them*. Hence the popular game known as faggies: a game in which you flicked cards alternately with an opponent, and he who flicked best won the pile of cards hitherto flicked. Actually, there were two varieties of the game, one with higher stakes than the other. In the less nerve-wracking game, you simply had to flick a card over your opponent's card, partially covering it; if you did this before your opponent did, you won all the cards. Usually there would be no more than ten cards flicked before someone got a hit. But in the other game there was scope for far greater wins and losses: here you had to knock over one or more cards propped against a wall, and the player who knocked over the last propped card won the whole lot. This was far more taxing as a skill and it was quite possible for a hundred cards to be flicked before someone emerged victorious. The adrenaline! The yelling! The essence of the skill lay in being able to launch the card fast and level, so that it cut sharply through the air, instead of fluttering impotently. To achieve the desired effect, you must use your index finger and its adjacent digit to grip the card by its corner and then give it a vigorous flick with plenty of wrist. Do this for half an hour straight and your forearm is hurting from the stress. This refined skill was particularly crucial in the knockdown version of faggies, and the thrill was to propel the flimsy missile in the direction of a propped card, skim it on the concrete and slam it into the target. You needed power and accuracy, with a light-speed wrist action. And you could play the game at variable, mutually agreed, distances, thus making it more or less demanding. Some cards were better than others for a strong, decisive trajectory, the thicker and newer the better; these were employed strategically. The thing is: it's incredibly hard to propel a card of those dimensions and mass with any force – much harder than with a playing card, say. If you get an average adult to try it, you will invariably witness a limp fluttering of the released card, with zero air-cutting power (no wrist, you see). I played the game obsessively at playtimes and after school, relishing both the physical skill and its material rewards (hundreds of pretty cards, neatly sorted into series). I used to practise at home every evening after school, on the linoleum against the bedroom door, for at least an hour, until I could *really* flick that thing. At one time – when I was around eight years old – I was the most feared faggies player in the school, and had won well over a thousand cards from my shattered schoolmates. But I had paid my dues to reach that dizzy apex; I had put the time in – I *worked* at it. Even now, fifty years later, I still have that flick down, but I'm probably half the player I was then (middle-age wrist, no doubt). The joy of unleashing that thin projectile into the air, watching it zoom in on its intended target, and then the propped card abruptly leaping into the air as it is struck by the incoming missile: this is an experience not to be missed. Then scooping up your opponent's cards, to be added to your already handsome collection: here was the pure thrill of victory.

As you can see, I was rather keen on faggies, although I mustn't short-change marbles and conkers. The thwack of a well-thrown marble on its quarry, sending it skittering away, and earning the right to make it yours: this also is a pleasure to be savoured. And the marbles themselves, with their brightly coloured interiors like little hearts, were a joy to behold (and hold); big white ones, in particular. And, naturally, swinging a tethered conker – deep brown, hardened, lethal – at someone else's dangling conker, striking it with full force, is also a moment of exquisite exhilaration. Shattering your opponent's prize conker all over the playground, so abrupt and irrefutable, leaving just the pointless knot on the end of his trembling string, is a consummation devoutly to be wished, although, of course, it may well be *your* prized conker that is thus reduced to fragments and ignominy. And conkers is actually quite a difficult skill to master: the harder you try to strike the target, the more likely you are to miss it, with your conker whipping smartly round to rap you painfully on the knuckles. Missing time and time again is a palpable humiliation, and you only get one go before your deadly opponent gets to swing his again. It takes practice, patience and finesse to do it properly, as well as a degree of brute force. And unlike marbles and faggies, the materials of the game are destroyed while it is being played. Conkers is a zero-sum game. It's all smash or be smashed.

Outside school I was a notorious enthusiast of the Dutch arrow (they weren't allowed in school, for reasons that will become plain).

I don't know if children make these any more, but if they don't they are missing out. You cut a piece of branch from a suitable tree (we thought hazel trees were the best – we also used to eat the nuts), about 30 cm long and 1 cm in diameter, nice and straight. Then you insert some flights made from playing cards at one end, having cut suitable slits for them to slide into, and sharpen the other end into a point. Next a groove is cut under the flights in order to provide a grip for the knotted string that will be used to propel the arrow. The string is tightened around the shaft of the arrow over the knot, drawn taut down its length, and the arrow is gripped with the string entwined around the fingers near the pointed end. When the arrow is launched the string acts as a catapult whose fulcrum is the shaft's groove, and far greater power is thereby imparted to the missile than by simply gripping it in the hand and throwing it. It takes skill to make a Dutch arrow, skill to get the string to grip the shaft in the right way, and skill to throw it. But when it is thrown right, it really soars. I remember fashioning a beauty when I was still less than ten years old, hardening the point with fire (making fires was another of my activities), fitting the flights just right, and going to my local park for its maiden flight. At the end of the field I could see a group of lads messing around, maybe eighty yards away; I decided to launch in their general direction – intending no harm, you understand. I drew my arm back, string taut, and hauled off: the arrow streaked into the air, took flight in the direction of the distant group, kept going and going, and finally landed in the *middle* of the group, the hardened point sinking an inch into the soil with the flights quivering. I watched with mounting panic during the few seconds it took for the arrow to arc towards them; I had no idea it would be *that* good. The startled boys recoiled in amply justified alarm as the arrow twanged into their midst, while I ran up to retrieve my lethal weapon. When I reached them I made no comment (never apologise, never explain), just casually yanked the arrow from the ground, as if nothing had happened, secretly thinking: I'd better be more careful in future. For all I know, Dutch arrows were banned from the British Isles soon after ("Man Speared by 'Dutch' Arrow. Small Boy Detained"). At any rate I haven't seen one in nearly fifty years, although I did make one for my nephews and nieces a couple of years ago – and it *still* soared. I also used to make bows and arrows, as well as regular catapults, but it was the Dutch contraption that really engaged me: the simple but ingenious design to harness power and enable the body to do what it was incapable of before. Throwing stones was OK, and I did plenty of that, but it didn't have the same magic. And it didn't involve serious *equipment*. Ingenious people, the Dutch.

I'm going to skip swings, slides and roundabouts, as well as tree-climbing, air-gun shooting and darts, because I want to get to my first really serious engagement with sport: gymnastics. That monkey business on the beam was a harbinger: from early on I liked to throw my body around, particularly using my arms. I *looked forward* to physical education (PE) lessons because I could work on my body-throwing skills. I mastered headsprings and handsprings early, and was an adept of the vaulting horse and box. I could hoist my body up a rope to the ceiling of the school gym using only my arms, with legs extended outwards. Front and back somersaults soon evolved. I learned to balance in several different poses on my hands, the most difficult being a horizontal balance on the palms with the body straight (which I can still do: you have to dig your elbows into your ribs to get the right equilibrium). How good was I at gymnastics? I was the best in the school, to be sure, but not much better than that: I don't think I could ever have competed at a serious level. In a school competition I came in a disappointing second to a boy not generally regarded as my superior. It was a case of nerves on my part and of my rival selecting moves of a lower degree of difficulty than mine, which I failed to perform perfectly. I found the loss hard to take, as I knew I was the better gymnast; but, you know, it was character building and all that. Did I compete hard enough on the day? We'll come back to that later, when I consider competition more directly. What matters is that I developed a passion for this kind of controlled movement, this muscular tussle with gravity. I could make my body do what I wanted it to: flip, bounce, jack-knife and cartwheel. I could make it *fly*. Gymnastics is surely the sport in which self-propelled flight is at its purest (consider, particularly, the high bar). You don't *have* to stand earthbound on two legs; you can put distance between yourself and terra firma.

Gymnastics led me to three other sports that are closely related: trampolining, diving and pole vaulting. These are all scary activities, in which you need to know your limits. It's easy to bounce clean off the trampoline and unless someone blocks your fall, you end up dropping from a considerable height onto the hard gym floor. Trampoline is a mixture of fear and exhilaration in equal measure. I was particularly fond of performing the twisting seat drop. I was good enough to win the Butlins trampoline open for boys under sixteen in 1965 or thereabouts (my younger brother and our friend came in second and third – a clean sweep). Diving also followed naturally, although hitting the water head first from a great height is not the most relaxing of experiences. I liked the springboard best, because of its gymnastic character, and also because the ten-metre board brought out my innate fear of heights (which I still have). I very much desired to be an outstanding diver but never progressed much beyond single front somersaults – I needed proper coaching, really. I had a nice smooth entry though, straight and splashless.

But the pole vault was my best event, by far. How to convey the thrill of sprinting down the runway, pole outstretched, planting it firmly in the box, feeling the momentum thrust you high in the air, and then dropping serenely and cleanly over the bar? It's like ... pole vaulting: nothing compares to it. The skill requires speed and power in the run-up, exquisite timing in the plant, an acrobatic upward thrust as feet rise above hands, and then the twist of the body as the pole is released, and the long lazy drop down. We used only rigid aluminium poles in those days, not flexible fibreglass poles, and I never vaulted higher than ten feet, but the thrill of gaining that much height from your own speed and skill was incredible. I was school champion and record holder, but in the town sports was easily beaten by a boy from another school who could do at least a foot higher than I could. But it wasn't the competition that attracted me; it was the thrill of the skill. It felt amazing to be able to do it at all. On the fear and danger side should be listed the following: missing the box with the pole and sliding on your back down the hard runway; tipping sideways at the apex of the vault and crashing into the uprights; falling backwards to the hard ground because of a lack of forward momentum; bouncing on the bar as you try to clear it and having it land on you afterwards. All these things happened to me at least once, and they were scary all right, and quite bloody too. But then, the clean, graceful vault, the inches of clearance, the *height* – that made it all worth while. To practitioners, it feels like the most natural thing in the world.

Lest you think I'm addicted to danger in sports, I must now move on to table tennis, my other main sporting passion in the early years. We had a table tennis table at home, in the garage, so I could practise as much as I liked. Moreover, my brother Keith, one year younger, was also a keen player (as were my parents). We played for hours and knew each other's game inside out: he defensive, I attacking. If you saw us play together, you would think we must be youth champions of some sort, so adept we were at returning each other's balls. I even had some coaching as a boy and learned how to hit shots correctly, with all kinds of spin. Nowadays, it pains me no end to miss shots I would have found so easy at fifteen. I would hit almost anything with a brisk forehand topspin, and particularly enjoyed thrashing overconfident adults. It was repeatedly *not missing* with fast topspin, backhand as well, that gave me particular pleasure. But it must be said that I enjoyed that style of play so much that I would stick to it even if it wasn't working for me. I'd sometimes rather lose than rein my game in. I enjoyed the spectacle too much for my own competitive good. (Some may say I'm the same way now in philosophy.) I also had a connoisseur's attitude toward bats, balls and nets, and I *hated* to play with a lousy bat. I always made sure I had a top notch bat to play with: fast rubber over sponge, sculpted grip, pricey. Anyone who despises "pingpong" as a serious sport needs to get to the table with someone who *really* knows how to play. It's soul shattering.

Ten pin bowling is also fairly risk free, and also not a skill to be despised in my view. Nor is it easy, not by a long chalk. The awful embarrassment of landing your ball in the gutter only half way down the lane! But the joy of that sudden convulsion which is a strike: the anticipation as your ball curves inexorably towards the pocket, the near-certainty of the strike, then the collective *thwock* as the pins lay each other low. Yes! Then the triumphant return to the seating area, away from the spotlight of the lanes, the simple and definitive X marked on the score sheet. But the thing with ten pin bowling is that you always feel like you're doing less well than you should be. What should have been a 200 game, at least, sputters out as a 136. You keep missing those easy spares. The strikes dry up unaccountably. If only you could just get those four short steps right, and swing the ball just so: *then* things would be perfect. But then you gutter it on a simple spare, or a sure-fire strike turns into an impossible split, and mortality rudely asserts itself. You always feel like a bum who could have been a contender in the unforgiving glare of the bowling alley. The Platonic bowler beckons, with his perfect 300 game, but he always seems to recede out of reach, like a distant rebuke. Every time you get a strike you think, *now I've got it*, and then your next ball is a total bust. There's a lot of swearing in bowling alleys, in case you haven't noticed. Bowlers always feel as though fate is against them. Still, at least I don't jog up to the lane cradling the ball like a baby and then simply drop it loudly on to the shiny wood and hope for the best – as it trickles into the gutter a couple of feet away. (In fact, I now have my own ball and shoes, and can put on a decent impersonation of a professional – if you don't watch where my ball goes.)

Pinball: I played that too, if "played" is the word. For a period, pinball was my *life*. There was a machine at the South Pier in Blackpool, called Sunset, which favoured the player who could *trap* the ball: catch it on the flipper, hold it still, then release it at just the right moment to strike the desired target. If you were really good at trapping, you could score free games on the Sunset at a heady rate, with each game won sounding like a gunshot. I once saw a boy from my school, nicknamed "Deadbrick" (Livingstone being his real name), who was particularly brilliant at pinball – although not at anything else – rack up twenty-six free games in a row off that machine. The trouble was, when you showed up at the pier with your cadged change, itching for a game, some other likely lad would be on there all night scoring one game after the other; there would literally be fist fights to see who would play next. The boys I knew in those days had trouble with the concept *taking turns.* It was truly amazing to witness the levels of skill and artistry that could be exercised on such a cheesy game, and the passion too. The Who's song "Pinball Wizard" sums it up perfectly, particularly the near-mystical reputations of the top players. I have never found a machine to match the Sunset and I yearn for it to this day. Pinball gets into your blood. Once addicted, never cured. It has been a steady occupation of mine for the past forty years, when the occasion arises. We are all recovering pinball wizards, me and the lads.

I also played my first tennis (about which much more later) in my teens. I used to play with my friend Andrew, who was by *far* the best all-round sportsman in my school, in the local park. We were always getting rained off, and the Blackpool winds were a hazard. I never took a lesson, learning my technique (such as it was) from watching Wimbledon on television, and I relied on quickness around the court. I wasn't bad considering that I had no real stroke proficiency, but there was an awful lot of whacking the ball out and general slashing around. Why did the ball keep going so high all the time? It wasn't until many years later that I began to repair this appalling gap in my athletic education. There are few things as infuriating as an inability to hit a tennis ball with accuracy and pace, and it pains me that so many years went by without my doing anything serious to get this deficiency rectified. The seed was sown, however, and tennis remained an intermittent fascination for me over the decades. If only it weren't so difficult!

At around this time, when I was fifteen or so, most of my friends started smoking, and urged me to join them (the perfect relaxation between manic pinball games). I'm sure my sporting interests were part of my reason for resisting, that and a perverse desire to flout peer pressure. It had just been announced that smoking causes lung cancer and I solemnly cited this as my reason for not starting. Smoking and sport just don't go together. You need your lungs. Admittedly, I had smoked my first cigarette at the age of nine, but my grand total during those early years was probably no more than ten (I was a two-a-year man). After the age of fifteen, it hardly seemed to me cool any more to smoke – been there, done that – and I've never held a cigarette between my lips since then (cigars and a pipe, yes, but only very moderately). Health and sport are obviously connected, and I prized my health even then.

How about the water? I'll have a lot to say about the water later, but during my early years I was water-phobic. There were two main reasons for this: I was nearly drowned when I was five; and the water was just too bloody cold. The former event occurred on a family trip to the coast near Margate: I got out of my depth while walking alone into the sea and was soon gulping down salt water until I became unconscious. I felt myself about to die, and very nearly did. It was an extremely nasty experience, to put it mildly; and understandably soured me to the joys of swimming. On top of that, the local swimming pools and the sea were just so cold, even in

11

the middle of summer; I could hardly stand to be in them for longer than five minutes at a time. I did eventually learn to swim, despite my phobia, at around eight or nine, but was poor at it, and unenthusiastic. The water felt to me like an encumbrance and a threat, rather than a liberating medium (even now swimming is something I can take or leave). My later passion for the ocean, which I shall come to in a later chapter, should be set beside this early negative experience. Drowning is something very real to me.

Then there was fishing, which I did as a teenager off the pier in Blackpool. I liked everything about fishing except the part involving the fish. I particularly enjoyed the *casting*: whipping the rod forwards with thumb on reel and releasing the lead weight with maximum velocity. I aimed for the greatest casting distance, the plop of the weight hardly audible from the pier. About the actual fish I was squeamish, and felt vaguely guilty about reeling them in. I also enjoyed the *worming* part of the total fishing experience: going out early in the morning with a specially designed worming spade to dig up the lugworm that we used as bait. This is a sport in itself, requiring skill and speed. You have to dig towards the worm cast in a special pattern in order to surprise the worm beneath the cold sand, or else it will burrow downwards at a great pace and you won't even see its tail. Who is faster, worm or man? If you dig right, you catch a glimpse of its back end and then hurl yourself face down into the deep wet hole you've just dug and grab it by the tail. But it would struggle mightily to break free of your grip, and often would. These were some fiercely resourceful worms, I can tell you, and slimy as hell. We boys were in awe of seasoned fishermen who would arrive at the pier with over a hundred worms dug that very morning; I'd usually have half a dozen after two hours of hard digging. Every sport has its trials and tribulations, I suppose.

I think I have assembled enough data now to venture some generalizations and analysis. This has not merely been a trip down memory lane. (I have omitted my various entanglements with football, cricket, basketball and discus, restricting myself to the sports that made the greatest psychological impact on me.) What philosophical themes can be extracted from my early experience with sport? What did it all *mean*? There are several questions to answer: how to define "sport"; the relationship between sport and education, specifically knowledge; the mind–body connection in relation to sport; the ethics and meaning of competition; the value of sporting activity. I have described my early sporting experiences with these broader themes in mind, so that now I can proceed to more abstract questions with a firm and varied empirical basis. My aim is to think about sport from the *inside*, as a participant not a spectator: to capture what philosophers would call the *phenomenology* of sport, that is, what it's like to do it. This is a far more helpful and illuminating perspective from which to approach the place of sport in human life than via the spectacle of it as passively viewed on the television screen. I'm not interested in the phenomenon of *watching* sport, viewing it as a non-participant outsider, but in *doing* it. I seek the first-person perspective.

First, definition: what do we mean by "sport"? When we seek a philosophical understanding of sport, what is it we are seeking an understanding *of*? It is evident from the list of sports I have mentioned so far – just a small subset of everything we call "sport" – that there is great variety in what can be so called. Some of the activities I've cited might even strike some readers as hardly *sports* at all. Conkers? Pinball? *Worming*? These might be described as "games" or maybe just "physical activities", but it's a stretch to call them all sports. I sympathize with this reaction; I wouldn't want to insist that everything I've described counts as a sport in any strict sense. The trouble here is that the concept of sport is simply not a precisely delineated concept. Where do sports leave off and games begin? When is an activity sport or merely exercise? Is competition essential to sport? Can you compete with something that isn't a human being – such as a river or a mountain? Must there be something that counts as winning and losing? How necessary is acquired skill to sport? Do animals engage in sport? Is all sport recreational? How much machinery can be used before an activity ceases to be a sport? How much bodily movement does there need to be? Is tiddlywinks a sport? Is sex? In view of conundrums like these, it seems to me folly to attempt a strict definition. We do better to follow Wittgenstein's lead in his treatment of the concept of a game. In a famous section of *Philosophical Investigations* he writes:

> Consider for example the proceedings that we call "games". I mean board-games, card-games, ball-games, Olympic games, and so on. What is common to them all? – Don't say: "There *must* be something common, or they would not be called 'games'" – but *look and see* whether there is anything common to all. – For if you look at them you will not see something that is common to *all*, but similarities, relationships, and a whole series of them at that. To repeat: don't think, but look! – Look for example at board-games, with their multifarious relationships. Now pass to card-games; here you find many correspondences with the first group, but many common features drop out, and others appear. When we pass next to ball-games, much that is common is retained, but much is lost. – Are they all "amusing"? Compare chess with noughts and crosses. Or is there always winning and losing, or competition between players? Think of patience. In ball games there is winning and losing; but when a child throws his ball at the wall and catches it again, this feature has disappeared. Look at the parts played by skill and luck; and at the difference between skill in chess and skill in tennis. Think now of games like ring-a-ring-a-roses; here is the element of amusement, but how many other characteristic features have disappeared! And we can go through the many, many other groups of games in the same way; we can see similarities crop up and disappear.

And the result of this examination is: we see a complicated
network of similarities overlapping and criss-crossing: sometimes overall similarities, sometimes similarities of detail.

(§66)

What Wittgenstein says of games applies equally to sports. Not
that the concept of sport and the concept of game are the *same*
concept: clearly chess, say, isn't a sport, and nor is the high jump
really a game. But both these concepts are held together, not by a
feature common and peculiar to all cases to which we apply the same
concept, but by what Wittgenstein goes on to call "family resemblance": a sense of overall similarity not analysable in terms of necessary and sufficient conditions. The best way to explain a concept like
this is by way of ostensive definition employing paradigm instances:
this (pointing to a tennis game) is a sport, and *that* (referring to high
jump) is also a sport, whereas the thing over *there* (a chess game) is
not a sport. In other words, we explain the concept of sport by saying
something like: tennis and high jump are sports, and *things like that*
are also sports – but we don't attempt to specify the *respect* in which
activities have to resemble tennis and high jump to be sports. The
concept of sport is an open-ended and negotiable concept, not
one that is precisely tied down to a uniform set of activities. This
is why there are debates about whether to include certain kinds of
activities in the Olympic Games: bodybuilding, windsurfing, ultimate fighting. There is no Platonic essence here, just a motley selection of more-or-less similar activities. Compare the concept of *art*,
which likewise includes a very wide variety of disparate activities
and products. Neither *sport* nor *art* are concepts with the precision
of *triangle* or H_2O. There is an inherent vagueness to the concept of
sport, and there may simply be no fact of the matter about whether
a given activity is or is not a sport (consider, say, darts).

So let's not trouble ourselves over questions of exact definition.
The concept of sport serves us well enough, despite vagueness

about its boundaries, and we can always focus on specific activities and not worry about how far the concept extends. In fact, my interest in this book extends to things we normally regard as games, as well as to sports proper. I'm interested in *skilled movement* of the kind typified by paradigm instances of sport (so not piano playing or drumming or typing). Just as there is something called "philosophy of science" without any agreed-on definition of what counts as a science, so we can develop a philosophy of sport without being able to provide a strict non-circular definition of the concept. For me, what is important is the acquisition of a physical skill, where this is typically both difficult and strenuous, and where something counts as success or failure. There will also characteristically be a means–end structure to the activity in question: there is something you are aiming at and there is a method for achieving it – hitting the tennis ball into the service area, jumping over the bar, reaching the finish line first, catching a wave while standing on a board, smashing someone else's conker and so on. There is an objective to the movement and there is a skilled way to achieve that objective. This means that the athlete always has in mind an ideal that she is trying to get her body to live up to, an intention she is trying to realize by means of the body (so there are no sports that can be played purely inside your head). In any case, I think you know what I am talking about, despite my inability to delineate it with mathematical precision.

What is it to acquire a sporting skill? When you learn a sport what has changed in you? Clearly, you can *do* something you couldn't do before. When I learned various gymnastic moves my body could do things it couldn't do before. This makes it tempting to describe sporting skill as purely *bodily*, that is, as removed from the mind or intellect. Such a conception excludes sport from the realm of the educational, since education is concerned with the acquisition of knowledge, and that, we think, is the province of the mind not the body. Then, learning a skill is properly described merely as training the body (as opposed to the mind). Skill is opposed to contemplation as the body is opposed to the mind. But this is clearly the wrong way to think about it: the mind is obviously deeply involved in learning sporting skills – there is intention, planning, effort, perception, judgement, "feel", exhilaration and so on. Above all, we should recognize that learning a sport is the acquisition of a certain type of *knowledge*, so that athletic education is not discontinuous with other kinds of education. There is no sharp dichotomy here. As a first step, let's note that the bearer of knowledge is the *person* not the mind: *I* know things – it is a category mistake to say that my *mind* knows things. And the person is a psychophysical unity – something that has *both* mental and physical attributes. Perhaps it is true that I know things *in virtue* of having a mind, but it is not true that all knowledge pertains only to the mental side of me and has no expression in my bodily nature. The person is the proper object of education, not just his or her mind, and the person is an embodied entity. So it is not an oxymoron to speak of "physical education", where this implies knowledge that expresses itself primarily in the body. The body can be a repository of knowledge, as well as the mind. *I* can know things that my *body* manifests, as well as things that subsist wholly in my mind.

Of course, this is really quite obvious, because we readily speak of *learning* a sporting skill, *knowing* how to play a game, *grasping* the nature of a particular action. I had to *learn* how to pole vault, and I came to *know* how it was done, and I *understood* the mechanics of it. This is what philosophers call *practical* knowledge or "knowing how", as opposed to *theoretical* knowledge, the kind you might have of physics or history or geography (sometimes called propositional or factual knowledge). When you pick up a sporting skill you acquire practical knowledge, in the sense that you acquire a specific ability with a cognitive dimension. It is not that you know the answers to various questions about a subject and can pass a written test, but that you can perform a certain task successfully.

This knowledge is expressed by your body, as other types of knowledge might be expressed verbally. But it is as much genuine knowledge as any other kind of knowledge, which means that physical *education* is not a misnomer. Physical education aims at knowing-how, as historical education aims at knowing-that. But both are kinds of knowledge, one no more than the other.

This point may strike you as obvious, but it helps to overcome a certain prejudice about the standing of sport. You see, I wasn't just wasting time when I spent all those hours in my early years on sports and games, diverting myself from the serious business of getting a decent education. I was in fact acquiring a whole lot of *knowledge*, and knowledge, as Plato insisted, is valuable in itself. Indeed, Plato strongly advocated the virtues of physical education, especially in gymnastics (which comes from the Greek word for "naked" – the Greeks did their athletics in the nude); and Plato regarded knowledge as the key value of the good life. He thought the highest knowledge was knowledge of the Forms, those abstract and perfect entities that exist outside the sensible world but that give it whatever reality it has. Perhaps he might have agreed that gymnastic knowledge gives you knowledge of your *own* "form" – of your own distinctive being as an embodied entity. It's not just "Know thyself", but also "Know thy own body". In other words, sporting ability is a type of bodily knowledge. I know my body *through* sport, as I know sport through my body. This is a distinctive type of knowledge, with its own preconditions and mode of expression, and perhaps its own distinctive value. The *prestige* we attach to knowledge therefore carries over to sport, because sport *is* knowledge. Those jocks might not be as dumb as we tend to think (at least when it comes to their own bodies). You can't perform a sport successfully without containing a good deal of knowledge, because athletic skill is knowing-how.

The kind of knowledge you have of a skill is typically not explicitly expressible: you can't say how you do it exactly, you just *do* it. This is sometimes called *tacit* or *implicit* knowledge, in contrast to the conscious and verbally expressible type of knowledge. Our knowledge of language is often characterized in these terms: we have tacit knowledge of the rules of grammar and sentence construction, not explicit knowledge that would enable us to state what those rules are. Likewise, when you have the ability to kick or throw a ball accurately, your knowledge is tacit; you certainly don't consciously know the principles of physics that go into the pace and trajectory of the ball. This is why often the best players are the worst teachers: they simply can't access the nature of the skill they so effortlessly exercise. The successful tennis coach is someone who knows explicitly what the likes of Roger Federer may know only implicitly, which is why the latter needs the former, despite his inferior skill. Not all knowledge exists "before the mind"; some lurks deep within the body, or in that strange and mysterious intersection of mind and body. In exactly what *part* of me did my knowledge of pole vaulting exist? In my whole being, one feels inclined to say: in the psychophysical unit that *I* am. It is artificial to say it resided in *either* my mind *or* my body. Similarly, for singing, dancing and driving a car.

In learning a sport there is very often – although not always – a curious transition from the explicit to the implicit. Someone tells you how to do it, and you think you get the idea: how to flick a fag card, say. But your body won't carry out what you think you know. So you practise and practise, until it starts to "sink in". After a while your body seems to take over and you perform the required action smoothly, even forgetting the explicit instructions that initially guided you. Here is where people speak of "muscle memory" as opposed to "mental memory": the motor system in the brain absorbs the know-how that earlier existed only in your conscious knowledge. Puzzling as this process is psychologically, it is surely one of the great satisfactions of learning a sport: that blissful moment when what you have laboured consciously to carry out, and failed so many times to enact, appears as a smooth and easy action, almost a reflex. You leave conscious thought behind and enter the realm of pure bodily skill (only to relapse ten minutes later, when you have to start focusing again). If only we could hand over all of life's tasks to this expert "unconscious"! There comes a point when you don't have to think about it any more; the burden of conscious thought has been lifted. Less has become more, epistemically speaking. This is brilliance without effort, genius without reflection. But only intense exertion in the learning phase can lead to such a release from conscious control. You become a natural player only by first being an unnatural one. Paradoxically, it is only when you stop "knowing" that you really *know*.

This bears on the old dualism of mind and body. In the learning phase of a sport, the dualism is experienced as real: the body refuses to do what the mind tells it to, and the mind is only too conscious of the problem. This is the *practical* mind–body problem: basically, how to convert intentions into movements, thoughts into actions. Here the body lags behind the mind, rebels against it even. But in the accomplishment phase no such duality is experienced; the person functions as a coordinated unit, a seamless whole. Acquiring athletic competence is thus a unification of mind and body, both real and felt. Cartesian dualism finds it hard to do justice to this kind of skill, because according to that view what is psychological belongs exclusively to the non-spatial mental substance, while what is bodily belongs exclusively to a mechanical system distributed in space. How then could my *body* know things? That must seem like a contradiction to a Cartesian. My mind knows things, not my body. The truth is that *I* know things, and I have both mental and bodily attributes; or better, the distinction between mental and bodily attributes becomes otiose in the realm of physical skill. Take serving in tennis: the natural verbal expression we use to attribute that skill would be "I can serve in tennis" or "I can place the ball with varying speed at different positions inside the service area". Is this a "mental" description or a "physical" one? Certainly, intention and knowledge play a crucial role, as also do the configuration and dynamics of the body, but the ability in question belongs to neither category separately: it is a unified quality that the person possesses. You couldn't have that quality in a disembodied state, and yet the mind is indispensable to the skill. I think that sport enables us to experience ourselves as a unity: mind and body don't just run in parallel, occasionally communicating messages to each other, some-times out of harmony, but they seize each other and generate a new unity – the embodied agent. Such experiences of unity are important to us, and I shall discuss them further later. The body is experienced not as an alien entity – as it so easily can be experienced in illness, clumsiness and sexual dysfunction – but as integral to us as a person, as constitutive of our agency. The body becomes an extension of the will, not its coefficient of resistance. In sport at its best the two sides of our nature become fused and harmonious. The seventeenth-century French philosopher René Descartes was obviously not much of a sportsman (he had trouble coordinating his mind and his body): he regarded the self as inherently disembodied, tenuously linked to the body in space, and that doesn't fit the experience of skilled movement.

That all sounds very well, you might say, but what of the dark side of sport? I have been speaking of sport as an exercise of skill, but isn't it usually an exercise of skill whose point is to *beat* the *opposition*? I want to speak more of competition in the next chapter, but here I should acknowledge some of the dangers of the adversarial character of competitive sport. In a competition someone has to lose, obviously, and losing doesn't feel too good; indeed, it can sometimes be quite devastating. I didn't enjoy losing the school gymnastics competition to that other boy one bit, especially as I disappointed myself on the big occasion (I still remember with shame that bungled back flip). Nor did my opponents at faggies enjoy having their prized cards taken from them. There is also the triumphalism that comes with winning, the disdain and pride, the love of power and domination. Isn't competitive sport inherently alienating? Doesn't it elevate the individual above the community? Where is the altruism in trying your best to savage someone else athletically? It's all "dog eat dog", the survival of the fittest, the stronger smashing the weaker (just look at all those professional athletes with questionable *moral* skills). These are all legitimate concerns, I concede, to which there is no quick and easy answer. What I want to observe now is that competition, although integral to many sports, need not be the defining characteristic of sport, its *raison d'être*. In particular, the happiness produced by sport need not consist solely, or at all, in the happiness *of winning*. To me, competition is incidental to sport, a means rather than an end, and in truth I rather dislike it as an overriding motive. Unprincipled competition is what has happened to sport under late capitalism, but the essence of sport isn't tainted by this intrusion into its purity. You can engage in sport while eschewing competition, and even when you compete you can do so in a morally acceptable manner. Competition need not result in the suspension of morality, but in its redeployment. But I shall speak more of this important matter later.

To be set on the positive side, sport feeds into friendship. Even when you are competing with someone, you are also cooperating with them, because without the other person there wouldn't be a game at all. (The enemy is the guy who takes his ball home.) You can only compete by *first* cooperating to get the competition going. You refer to your tennis "partner", even though you are trying to wipe him out on the court. And whenever you play with someone else you are participating in an activity you both value, even love; you are sharing something with another human being. To be a good partner you have to comport yourself in the proper manner: you have to be *sportsmanlike*. People won't play with you if you behave badly. Playing sports with others teaches the art of friendship, and obviously friendships are often formed in this way. The person on

the other side of the net is not your enemy; he is the precondi-
tion of your being on the court at all, exercising your skills. When
I played tennis with my friend Andrew there was no bracketing of
our friendship; we engaged in "friendly competition". Jesus Christ
exhorted us to love our enemies; that's a pretty tall order for most
people, but I can see the point of counselling us to love our competitors in sport. There's no record of Jesus enjoying a lively game of
soccer with his disciples ("Go for it, Judas!"), but it would have been
a good opportunity to teach people to be ethical while trying to
outplay each other.

I have drifted into discussing the *value* of sport – why it is worth
engaging in – and that is really what this book is all about. It's about
why sport is valuable and what enhances its value (as well as what
reduces it). I am clearly not a disinterested spectator, viewing an
alien form of life from afar and wondering why people engage in
such a peculiar activity. To me sport is an essential part of the good
life, of the life worth living. Art, science, sport: all three matter (and
more besides). So I am here as an advocate. I also think it's important to dwell on the details of specific sports and not proceed at an
overly abstract level; just as a philosophical discussion of art would
be arid without reference to specific art works. As we proceed, I
shall introduce other sports that have preoccupied me over the
years, indicating how they figured in my life and what I derived
from them. Another author might make a different selection, but
some universal themes are bound to emerge. I sensed the value of
sport early on, suspended underneath that beam, and ever since I
have been tapping into it, one way or another.

2. Running up escalators

Until I was eighteen, sport played a large, even dominating, part in my life (music was my other passion). I was a scholar of movement. My PE teachers expected me to become a PE teacher myself, because I was clearly mainly interested in sport and also not too shabby with the book thing. They seemed nonplussed when I announced I was going to university to study psychology (where's the excitement there?). But my intellectual life took off around this time and the opportunities for sport were not as routinely available at university as they were at school. The result was that at university sport largely vanished from my life, to be replaced by books, late nights and sitting around all day drinking coffee. I did on a couple of occasions tag along with a friend who was involved in university gymnastics, but three things put me off: the skin peeling off my palms while practising on the high bar; being hit in the mouth and breaking a tooth while *supporting* someone else; and all the talk among the student gymnasts about broken backs. Studying the mind seemed much safer. I would still trot out my serial headsprings or my horizontal balance – mainly to impress the girls – but systematic sport disappeared from my life for about four years. It was nerd time for me. I suppose I needed to get my career together, as well as my love life, and it was the late 1960s and early 1970s, when sport was not much appreciated culturally; in any case, I let it go. A little table tennis here, some pinball there, maybe a round of darts: that was about the size of it (tremendous amount of talking, though).

However, in graduate school, at Oxford, I discovered squash. The nice thing about squash, from the British perspective, is that, being an indoor game, you can't get rained off: the bane of British tennis. The other nice thing is that the learning process is relatively rapid; you can get to a decent level in a short time. This means you have the *illusion* of being a competent player from early on, unlike with tennis, where incompetence dogs your every step. In squash you can hit the inelastic ball hard and not have it fly out of bounds all the time, and the kinetic energy quickly leaves the ball as it bounces off the walls and floor. If you have any racquet skills at all, you can start enjoying squash pretty much right away (I'd also played some badminton in earlier years, which helped). I enjoyed the vim and vigour of the game, especially striking the small un-bouncy ball with maximum power. It suits somebody slight and quick, like me. But squash is a sweaty claustrophobic game, cut off from nature, noisy and harsh. I used to play with another graduate student (name forgotten) at the Jesus College squash courts, and we had some highly enjoyable sessions in there, usually on a Sunday morning. I got tolerably good. I certainly never thought of it as "exercise" or "keeping fit"; to me it was pleasure, not prudence. I anticipated each game with excitement, that tingling feeling in the arms and legs, dying to swing and strike. I loved to whack my serve at my opponent, especially when it didn't come back.

But squash has its dark side, which brings us to the contentious topic of competition, which I broached in the previous chapter. Since squash is played in a tightly confined space, and at a hectic and violent pace, it is necessary to keep away from your opponent as he goes for his strike. But the more space you give him to move and swing, the more advantage he has over you. If you stand close behind him, he can't see where you are and you're then well placed to make the next shot. My partner had started standing closer and closer to me, as our games became more skilled and competitive. This had the effect not only of giving him an edge, but also of inhibiting my stroke for fear that I might hit him with my racquet. I, on the other hand, was far too afraid of being hit myself to crowd him in this way. One day the inevitable happened: he was standing close behind me, invisibly, and as I swung, my racquet struck him square in the mouth, breaking one of his front teeth. The blood, the sudden silence, the apologies: you can picture the scene. I liked him, he was a friend, so I felt very bad to have injured him in this way, but we both knew where the real blame lay (I believe I had had words with him before about the perils of his positioning). He needed a new front tooth. Our later games were far more tentative, and ethically tinged, with him sensibly keeping his distance and me constantly afraid I might hit him again. I count this a very unfortunate experience for both of us: his tooth, my conscience. It took much of the fun out of the game. This was a conflict between safety and competitiveness, and safety came in second. To me, injuring someone, or being injured by them, in the course of excessive competition is the height of foolhardiness. Winning isn't worth it.

That wasn't the only squash injury I've been party to. Some years later, when I was teaching at University College London, I started playing a graduate student of mine (name withheld). He didn't have much natural athletic talent (he was a philosophy grad student after all) but he was determined and wily – and competitive. One day on the court I found myself in front of him in the middle of the court, directly in the line of fire. I tried to scramble out of the way so that he could place his shot. He struck the ball hard with me only feet away and facing him; and the ball went straight into my right eye. I dropped to the floor expecting to see my eyeball in front of me with blood pouring from the socket. In that moment I was certain I'd lost my eye. The ball had struck my eyeball with great force, one small globe in collision with another, and pushed it back into its orbit: the blow wasn't softened by surrounding bone – it was a direct hit. Amazingly, however, I could still see out of it, although blurrily, and it hadn't burst; and in the next few days my vision slowly returned to normal, although with a notable black bruise all around the socket. I can tell you, I wasn't happy with that, or with him. Bruised ego is one thing; bruised eyeball is quite another. My too-competitive partner should never have taken that sort of risk: he should have hit the ball off to the side or not at all or softly. But he saw a chance to win an easy point and neglected to consider the consequences of hitting someone in the face with a squash ball from close range. Again, excessive competitiveness was to blame: morality eclipsed by the desire to win. Sure, it was an accident – he wasn't *trying* to hit me in the eye – but in dangerous games you do what you can to avoid accidents. He did feel bad about it, certainly, but did he draw the right moral? I'm not sure. Competition is like that: virtue can easily dissolve in its white heat. Prudence, too.

Here's the obvious truth: it's not worth winning if you do it by fouling, cheating, risking your health or that of your opponent, or even trading on his psychological weaknesses – such as, say, his sensitivity about his mother's virtue. Intimidation, trash-talking, cheap shots: none of it is morally acceptable. It's not acceptable in big-money professional sports, and it's certainly not acceptable in games between "friends". The rule shouldn't be what you can get away with, but what counts as fair and decent behaviour. The referee is not your moral compass; you are. My own view is that the aliena-tion essentially bound up with winning and losing requires an espe-cially responsible attitude towards questions of fair play and human decency. Your moral sensitivity should be heightened, not lowered. If you're going to beat someone at something he badly doesn't want to be beaten at, at least have the goodness to treat him with respect and consideration. I don't even hold with fist-pumping and gleeful shouting when a point is won, or glaring at the opponent when you take a point from him (I'm thinking particularly of tennis here). End-zone dances are a disgrace. Off-the-ball fouls are an abomination. Jersey-tugging is intolerable. If you're playing tennis with a friend and a minor injury makes a particular shot difficult for him, it is *not* gentlemanly to exploit that weakness in his game. These are elementary truths in the ethics of sport, routinely violated as they are. And the problem is that the value of winning has come to trump other values integral to sport, such as fair play. The moral psychology of sport has become warped when victory counts for more than integrity. All that stuff about nice guys finishing last is pernicious rubbish. It is of course *not* true, contrary to a popular sentiment, that all's fair in love and war, and it's certainly not true in competitive sports. Victory is hollow when enabled by vice. The concept of *honour* is essential. (If you think this sounds old-fashioned, you're right: I follow the ancient Greek philosophers in moral matters.)

The right way to think of competition, of winning and losing, is as a means to a further, and higher, end: the pursuit of sporting excellence. Competition brings out the best in the skills and character of the players. I don't think you can complain if you just played the best tennis of your life and still lost the match. Equally, if you played ineptly and managed to win the game by luck and grind you should feel humbled; you didn't *deserve* to win. This is why tennis players always apologize for a net cord trickle-over: it was luck not skill that decided the point. If such a shot were possible intentionally, so that everyone had the chance to master it, then no apology would be needed; it would just be among the available resources of the game. The aim of competitive sports is not to win *tout court*, it is to win *justly*: fairly, by the rules, using only one's skill and power. As Plato would say, the just man does not stoop to defeat his opponent by unjust methods. As Kant would put it, you can't universalize the practice of cheating, affirming that *he* should cheat given that *I* do. As I would prefer: for Christ's sake, play fair! Indeed, you don't really *win*, except purely formally, if you defeat your opponent by unfair methods. You may be declared the winner, but you both know that your "winning" is a sham. It is a kind of lie: you merely pretended to play by the rules. You broke the implicit contract of the game. To engage in a competitive sport is to make a promise to play by the rules, so breaking them is breaking a promise. Simply trying not to get caught is something else entirely: it is doing wrong in the hope of not being held accountable. Don't get me wrong, it's not that I don't like winning: but not at the cost of losing my moral character. After all, moral victories are the sweetest kind. And let's not forget the ethics of losing: with good grace, with no excuses, sincerely congratulating the winner (no limp perfunctory handshake with zero eye-contact). The loser may feel sore inside, devastated even, but he must divorce his exterior from his interior and put on a good face. If the competition was fair, he can have no *moral* complaint.

If winning were all that mattered, you would choose opponents you could easily beat, thus chalking up a lot of effortless victories. But your game wouldn't improve much thereby, and your character wouldn't either. You need to play people roughly at your level, maybe a little higher, so that your game is continually improving: so that sporting excellence is the outcome. Unless you lose a good deal of the time, you will not be playing at your highest level. And let me make a point here about sexism, which should also be obvious: contrary to many a male ego, there is no shame in "losing to a girl", even a girl-"girl". I don't like to think about the number of times a talented female tennis player has felt it necessary to modify her game so as not to "embarrass" her male opponent. Come on, guys, shape up! You should *like* losing to a woman. At the very least, it gives you a chance to prove that you are no male chauvinist pig. I would love to be thrashed at tennis by a nifty nine-year-old lass (and I'm sure there are many out there who could do the job); I mean it. Recently, in fact, I was given a tennis lesson by a ranked twenty-seven-year-old female player, who vastly outclassed me, and it was the best twenty minutes of tennis I've ever had. People who avoid sports because they can't bear the prospect of losing need to do some serious soul-searching.

Speaking of competition, I had quite enough of that in my work life. I was a young man working as a professional philosopher, in an environment rife with rivalry, and it would be naive to suppose that I was under no competitive pressure. But there is a difference between athletic competition and the professional kind, or rather several differences. In sports there are rules of competition, penalties for infringements of those rules, referees and clear outcomes; but in career competition none of this holds. It's much easier for favouritism, discrimination, cheating of one kind or another, to go unidentified and unpunished. Sport is one area in which historically oppressed people can make their way, since there are public criteria for judging who performs the best. But in academic life, say, not to mention political and cultural life, where consensus opinion counts for so much, it is much easier to keep worthy people down. In a running race you cross the tape first and you win, simple, but where is the analogue of crossing the tape when it comes to presenting a good paper at a conference? It's always possible to say it wasn't that good really, if you don't like the person giving it. The opportunities for unjust competition are far greater when the rules are not so clear-cut. In particular, social background and "pedigree" play a negligible role in athletic contests (at least once everyone is allowed to compete), because the rules themselves make it clear who is the winner and the loser. Black athletes have enforced meritocracy in the sports world, where they could make little progress in the world of work. Once they were allowed to compete against white athletes, it often became only too clear who came out superior. Prejudice doesn't stand much chance against the stopwatch, the measuring tape and the score sheet. This is one of the great merits of sport as a social leveller. And the monetary rewards of top professional athletes have further strengthened the position of those heretofore discriminated against.

For me, at least, competition is a small part of the sports experience, and it is certainly not my motive for engaging in sports (I *love* it in philosophy, though – just kidding!). I would never defend athletics training as a necessary preliminary to competing in the world of work: the common idea that we learn to compete on the field and then bring that skill to other contexts (the seminar, the boardroom). The competitive spirit that is often held to be at the heart of capitalism – or sexual success for that matter – is not for me what sport is all about. It is more of a regrettable necessity than the essence of the activity: what makes you improve, rather than the whole point of the exercise. Weak players with a lust to win, but who never work to perfect their technique, always strike me as rather ridiculous, unless that lust gets channelled into improvement. For me, sport is about the development of the self, not the domination of others' selves, as I hope will become evident as we go on. Where is the glory in beating people even more mediocre than you are yourself? Excellence should be your aim, not beating this guy or that. Winning may be an *index* of excellence, but it cannot be constitutive of it (except perhaps at the very highest levels). Not that I disapprove of egotism in sports: standing out, looking good, gaining admiration. It is misplaced puritanism to suppose that sport, like other human institutions, should be purged of ego. Ego is a perfectly healthy motive, and I'm quite happy to cop to it. But ego is gratified by excellence, not by poor play that is marginally less poor than your rival's. By all means, let's be Nietzcheans about sport, but let's set the goals high. Be the best you can be, not merely better-than-him-over-there.

If my athletic activities were at best sporadic during my years as a student, they declined almost to zero when I started my first teaching job. I was twenty-four then, slim, fit, and not much different physically from what I had been at the height of my teenage athleticism. I had a lot of physical energy to burn and not much outlet for it. I recall that my main athletic activity was running up escalators on the London Underground (I'm not counting sex). I always wore trainers then, and when I was at the bottom of an escalator with not too many people on it, I would bound up the steps two at a time and refuse to be out of breath at the top, not breaking my stride as I levelled out. In general, I never walked up stairs, not me: I always ran up, gazelle-like, two at a time, sometimes three. There is skill as well as stamina to this (and ego, admittedly) – although to my knowledge there is still no Olympic event of escalator-ascent. If you are clumsy, you can trip and hurt yourself, and you have to glide smoothly and safely past the becalmed stationary ascendants (those immobile anti-athletes). It wasn't exactly pole vaulting, but it was something, this upward streaking. No one I knew participated in sports anyway and I always seemed busy with work, or hanging out at the pub. I'd play darts once in a while, as a break from working on philosophy, and there was always pinball to fall back on – the elevated realm of pub athletics. Otherwise, I lived the life of a typical sedentary academic: the gymnastics were all in my head. Walking was the most active thing I did, but I was usually talking at the same time, non-stop. There was some Frisbee in the park, I seem to recall, but nothing to break a sweat over. It was all desk, library and seminar room.

And what was the result of this period of lethargy and languor? A pot belly, obviously – what else? It had been growing for a while – furtively, trying to stay under the radar – but I noticed it with full force one day while in a shop changing room: a white mass mushrooming over my belt, soft, convex, *wobbly*. I wasn't exactly fat, you understand, but my erstwhile waspish waist was now a cladding of dough, with those frightful "love handles" perched on either side. In my gymnast days I would do push-ups, sit-ups and other ups on a daily basis; but now my chest was sunken, my shoulders sloped and my belly sagged. True, I'd published a few philosophy papers by then, maybe even a book or two, but that was thin consolation for the horror of what I confronted in the mirror: a belly as bloated as Kant's *Critique of Pure Reason*. I had a bad case of Philosopher's Torso. How bad is this going to get, I wondered, with me only in my mid-thirties at the time. I had seen what impending middle age could do to the human frame and it was not good. This was *not* my image of myself.

So I started running, and not just up escalators. By this time I had moved back to Oxford, as Wilde Reader in Mental Philosophy, and I lived near a park on a quiet street in north Oxford. I remember my first effort, the only running (apart from those escalators) I had done in over fifteen years. I had bought some proper running shoes and shorts (I hadn't worn shorts in a long time) and was ready to start getting my waistline under control. I started off quite briskly, sprinting down the Woodstock road in the late afternoon, but after about three minutes I was suffering badly and had to slow down. It's amazing how constricted and painful your lungs feel when you bring them out of retirement. I didn't give up, though, oh no. The entire run lasted about twenty minutes and when I returned home I felt like pure hell. My breathing was terrible, my legs were hurting and my stomach didn't look an inch narrower. Out of shape? I should say so. That, as they say, was my wake-up call. It took at least thirty minutes to get my breath back and feel more or less normal again. And then there was the next morning, with my legs feeling as if they had been beaten with bats. I decided then and there that I didn't care much for running, but that wasn't going to stop me. Run I would. I began running almost every day, pain or no pain. Of course, it got better, although it was never a pain-free experience and always called for a serious effort of will. I soon began to run longer distances, faster, harder and without muscle trauma the next day. My weight did start to drop (I was also dieting): the belly bulge looked more sheepish now, less confident of its place in the world. So it was working, but I can't say I ever *enjoyed* it. You see, running is exercise, not sport. There's a distinction (sorry, running, but you know it's true). Your skills don't measurably improve, only minimal coordination is required and the purpose of it is to improve fitness not to excel at some specific skilled activity. It's like quick walking, with a jogging motion to it. This is surely why academics prefer running as their chosen form of physical activity: you don't need any athletic ability to do it, just determination. It's work, not play.

Running is a little like studying for exams: an inherently painful process whose justification is entirely instrumental – passing the exam or getting fit (or at least not fat). I thought of running as distinctly interim: I'd run until I lost the weight and regained my fitness, and then I'd think of something else to do – something more *fun*. But what would that be?

I also started doing push-ups and sit-ups, after a ten-year break, acquiring weights to do other forms of upper-body exercise. It felt like reconnecting with my youth. And yes, there was a marked improvement in my physique, and my sense of well-being. But there was nothing particularly game-like or athletic about any of this. It was prudence not play: warding off the tubby spectre I'd glimpsed in that changing-room mirror. The only things that answered to the playful side of me at this time were video games, which for a while I played obsessively. First it was *Ms Pacman*, then *Galaga* and finally the all-consuming *Defender*. Here you compete with a machine, and you invariably lose. Those machines are *killers*. The physical side of it amounts to tapping buttons and pushing small levers, so not aerobically very challenging, but the adrenaline rush is real enough. They are an extension of pinball, only electronic not mechanical, and far more addictive. They invade your nervous system, taking up residence in the cortical folds. If your brain is a computer, they are a virus. Martin Amis wrote a book in the 1980s called *Invasion of the Space Invaders*, in which he describes the addiction these games produce, and the "wallet-thinning" conse-quences of that addiction. I can testify that *addiction* is the right concept here: the cravings, the excessive spending, all that hanging out in seedy joints ("amusement arcades", ha ha). Video games make faggies look classy in comparison. *Defender* alone nearly reduced me to haggard poverty (I exaggerate slightly). Even now, if I come across a *Galaga* machine in an airport – and they are making a sinister comeback – I'll want to have a "quick game" and I end up feeding coins in for as long as I can get away with. I can hear the characteristic lilting jingle of *Galaga* in my head as I write this, and the little chirp that signals that another stage is about to begin (here they come!). It doesn't surprise me at all that after these relatively primitive beginnings video games are now one of the biggest industries on earth. They tap into some submerged portion of the brain that has been waiting millennia for its proper exploitation. What would Freud have made of them (oral, anal, genital, *arcade-al*)?

This is a good point at which to address another potential danger of sport: obsession and addiction – otherwise known as training hard. I don't think I've ever played a game or participated in a sport with any seriousness and not become obsessed with it. People do. If you're not careful, it's all you think about. Do you suppose that the best players in the world at their chosen sport are anything less than totally absorbed in that sport? Monomania is normal and only to be expected: a *sine qua non* even. And the thing about obsession is that it leads to neglect – of everything else. Isn't there the danger with any sport that exposure to it might lead to addiction and to corresponding neglect of everything else? You become a "tennis junkie", a "gym rat", a "hockey nut", a "foosball freak". You can't live without it. Everything else seems to pale in comparison. You are *hooked*. Well yes, there is that danger – a very present one, too. But then, aren't there also philosophy addicts and physics freaks? Or cooking crazies and music maniacs? They too may neglect their families, become one-sided, fall into unhealthy life styles. Anything judged worthwhile by its participants can lead to excess. The answer is not to ban all such activities, or steer clear of them for fear of succumbing to a Siren song. The answer is to moderate their influence on you: to try to *strike a balance*. Not that this is easy – life isn't. There have certainly been times when I've let my life become too dominated by philosophy – all of it (a bit like the worming enthusiasm of my youth, I suppose). And balancing values that are incommensurate is particularly problematic (values that can't be compared on the same scale). How much time should I give to family and friends and how much to work? How much effort should I put into educating my mind and how much into my body? Which is more important, tennis or surfing? It's interesting that we use the word "balance" in two connections: as a conflict between forces leading to physical equilibrium, and as a type of temperament or life style. When you have a problem of balance in your life, you are subject to conflicting forces that threaten to throw you out of equilibrium: you might *fall*. One of these forces might be an enthusiasm for a particular sport, and this might conflict with family obligations or career advancement or friendship or financial wisdom. Each of these things is valuable, although not necessarily in the same way or for the same reasons, and there is only so much energy and time available. How much of your life resources should you put into sport at the expense of other pursuits? How much is too much?

It depends partly on where your talents lie, obviously. If you are a naturally gifted athlete, it makes sense to put more effort into that; if you're the brainy type, then certainly don't neglect the classroom in order to whack balls around. (If you're both, you have a problem – use your judgement, I say.) It also depends on opportunity. My own rough rule of thumb is to do something physically active at least three times a week for at least an hour. In an ideal world, I'd do a lot more than that. But I have other calls on my time, and it gets tiring doing sports all day. In Plato's day, the gymnasium was a place where physical training took place, as well as intellectual discussion and artistic productions (not to mention bouts of pederasty). That seems a wise arrangement to me: try to integrate these different aspects of the good life; don't compartmentalize them. I find that after a few hours of intellectual work I'm ready for some physical activity, and it would be nice if I didn't have to travel far to find partners and facilities. But I do think we have to be careful of excess in sports, because sport is very appealing. Plato also thought, despite his advocacy of gymnastic education, that the person who concentrates too exclusively on sport will become crude and philistine;

while the person who never gets up and moves will be soft and ineffectual. In the *Republic* we read:

> "Have you noticed," I asked, "how a lifelong devotion to physical exercise, to the exclusion of anything else, produces a certain type of mind? Just as a neglect of it produces another type?
>
> "What do you mean?"
>
> "One type tends to be uncivilized and tough, the other soft and over-sensitive, and ..."
>
> "Yes, I have noticed that," he broke in; "excessive emphasis on athletics produces an excessively uncivilized type, while a purely literary training leaves men indecently soft."
>
> (Part III, Book II)

We are all too familiar today with the "jock" mentality, or lack thereof, which seems to have been as prevalent in Plato's day as it is now; just as we are familiar with the bodily unease of the dedicated "nerd". Obviously, both mind and body must be nurtured and developed, with the proper amount of time and energy devoted to each. At different times of life, different proportions may be appropriate, depending on priorities, but surely a life that neglects either dimension will be impoverished. We must attend to our entire nature as psychophysical beings. We don't want to be uncivilized toughs, but we also don't want to be effete weaklings. As Aristotle would no doubt insist, we need to find the mean between the extreme jock and the out-and-out nerd. Then we will have *eudaimonia* (roughly, true happiness, full flourishing). Sport develops our bodily nature as discussion develops our mental nature.

I have said nothing so far about spectator sports. People in America often ask me if I have taken up an interest in American sports – football, baseball and basketball. They don't mean whether I play them; they mean whether I *watch* them. "Not really," I reply.

"Oh," they continue, "I guess you like to stick with rugby, soccer and cricket" (wry smile at this point). "No," I say, "I never took much interest in those either – watching them, that is". Here they look bewildered and change the subject (the question no doubt on their minds is "How do you feel about ballet?"). And it's true. Despite my sporting interests, I don't watch those kinds of sports on television (although I do watch a good bit of television). I will watch the World Cup and I sometimes watch the Super Bowl, but watching the weekly games of the local teams leaves me cold. The sports I like to watch are broadcast more rarely: gymnastics, athletics and tennis. Basically, I like to watch what I play or have played. That way I connect my watching with my doing. Most spectator interest in sports strikes me as tribal and nationalistic. You support "your" team, often hating their rivals and the rivals' supporters. I find this primitive and stupid, to be blunt, and we know where it can lead. I don't even want to sully the page with reports of "football hooliganism" and the like ("savages at a soccer match" would be less euphemistic). Sport in this sense is largely of negative value, and I hold no brief for it. And isn't it clear that the interest in sport, here, is centred on winning and losing, not the appreciation of athletic excellence? This is why the typical "fan" is so downcast when "his" team loses, even if they put on a great show, only to lose to a team even greater. If the spectators like the sport so much, I want to ask, why don't they play it themselves? The reason is that they don't really love the sport at all, only its trappings and (dubious) symbolism. Maybe I'm being too harsh: maybe you could love the sport of baseball, appreciate its subtleties and skills, while never once having the desire to hit a baseball yourself (I have hit a few myself at the batting range and thoroughly enjoyed it – nearly bought a bat). But typically, it seems to me, the kind of sports fan that I have in mind is sublimating his own thwarted desire to be a sporting hero – to be *somebody* – into the passive experience of watching others, while relishing just a little too much the victories of his team over other teams.

There is really nothing significant that unites the guy sprawled on his couch bawling his team on through inhalations of beer, on the one hand, and the guy who gets out on the field and actually gives it a go, on the other. I applaud the latter, but the former strikes me as pretty pathetic. That isn't sport; it's borderline psychosis. When sport becomes entwined with pathological worship of country or race or tribe or ideology, it is dragged into a vortex of delusion and insanity. Like many of the most inherently elevated things, it can be thoroughly debased (I'm thinking mainly of religion, which institutionalized sport can come to resemble). In any case, I don't recommend it. To be a lover of sport, as I am, is not to be one of those fanatics who stand on the sidelines and scream their heads off. This book is not written for them. Not that there is anything wrong with being a spectator as such: sport is, among other things, a spectacle, and it's only natural that people should enjoy such a spectacle. There is obvious pleasure to be had in watching a team sport and appreciating the intricacies and excitement of the game; and I'm not against cheering when a goal or a touchdown is scored. My complaint is against the kind of spectator who views sport as an opportunity for violence and hatred, or who invests his sense of self-worth in the performance of "his team". Also, it seems peculiar to me that anyone would want to watch what they have no interest in doing. My interest in this book is with sport as something you engage in, not something you merely observe.

3. Muscles, mountains and Manhattan

I started my running in Oxford, past those dreaming spires, damp and ancient. My usual route took me through University Parks, rain or shine, round the back of Magdalene College, where the deer gather, and back home again to Bardwell Road. I would do about thirty minutes at a decent clip, most days. I had my companions in locomotion, pounding around the park. I recall a short Asian fellow, probably a graduate student in one of the harder sciences, pushing himself ridiculously hard, always with a look of absolute agony on his contorted face, short thick legs pummelling the ground. We'd nod respectfully at each other. I wasn't prepared to go that far, but it wasn't a leisurely jog for me; I ran close to my limit (although my Asian friend might disagree). I always speeded up at the end to extract the remaining reserves of energy. I inhaled that Oxford air, moist and peaty, deep into my heaving lungs. Afterwards I hit the weights for twenty minutes in my bedroom. I was the Wilde Runner in Physical Philosophy, among other dedications. Physical exertion was back in my life and hasn't left it since.

I continued my running in Manhattan, past glowering towers, brash, modern, closely packed – first when I was a visiting professor there in 1988, and later when I moved there permanently. From 1990 I lived on the Upper West Side, quite near the Hudson River, just off Broadway, wide and teeming. My typical run began at 86th Street and went up to Columbia University at 112th Street, along Riverside Drive, the Hudson at my shoulder. It took about forty intense minutes, with hills and dells, and traffic stops, and came in at about five miles. In my brief runner's shorts and singlet I'd endure the witty comments of loitering individuals with nowhere else they'd rather be (i.e. homeless people). Sometimes I'd run round the Reservoir in Central Park for a change of scenery, although it tended to be more crowded there – and fashion conscious. I worked myself pretty strenuously most days, not wanting to loiter with the loiterers. I became quite good at running, although I never ran with much pleasure or even sense of satisfaction. My legs became efficient little machines. I could put one in front of the other quite quickly and for a fairly long time. It was utilitarian: to keep the weight off and the stomach in. I didn't want to see that reflection ever again, the one in the changing room (let's not wallow in the details). And it wasn't bad for thinking, and a little sightseeing. It kept me on the streets.

But there was the weather issue: too hot in the summer and too cold in the winter. To face scorching humid city heat and run through it – even the breeze seemed hot – was non-trivially unpleasant; it would take me an hour to stop sweating afterwards. I had friends who would run in the early morning to avoid the worst of the heat, but that never suited me: late afternoon was my preferred time. In the winter I'd have to pile on the thermal gear – gloves, hat, long trousers and jacket – and brave the searing winds off the river, usually in the dark. Often I'd be running on packed ice. That was none too pleasant either. Autumn and spring were OK, brief though they were, but there was still the strain of running itself. My face may not have been horribly contorted, but it was never beatific either (have you ever seen a smiling runner?). I never suffered from knee problems, but friends of mine did, and eventually had to give up running. So, to sum up and recapitulate, running in New York is not the most fun way to spend your time. There is, furthermore, a structural problem, a problem of mass distribution: your legs get strong but your upper body shrinks – you get runner's torso. Toned you may be, low in body fat, but the bulk is drastically reduced. That didn't suit me, as an ex-gymnast. (Still, it's better than what some trainers call "carb face".) I liked some muscle on my bones. What do you think I should have done?

Right, I joined a gym: Equinox on Amsterdam Avenue, which was just opening. This was a boom time for gyms in New York City: the *Zeitgeist* had declared that everyone had to be a member of a gym, grandmas included. The most immediate benefit was climatic: air-conditioned, temperature-controlled, with no more of the furnace and the refrigerator to contend with – plus an abundance of babes, naturally. Now I did my running on a treadmill, surrounded by like-minded individuals, at a steady temperature and humidity. I had entered the gym world, the gym cosmos (lots of circling stars and other heavenly bodies in various stages of development). In addition, we had all the fancy weight machines to grapple with; I soon became their intimate. It gets personal when you lock limbs that often and that strenuously. I flexed and grimaced in their embrace. This was the beginning of fifteen years of regular "working out" in the gyms of New York. The gym became like a second home to me. Later I joined the newly built New York Sports Club on Columbus Avenue, where trainers manhandle suffering celebrities in front of plush mirrored walls and animal grunts are forbidden (the Vatican has fewer rules). Six floors, a pool, two basketball courts, acres of hardware. My usual routine started with a two mile run on the treadmill, then weight training with machines and free weights, and finally thirty minutes on the stationary bike, watching a television perched on the opposite wall. The emphasis shifted from running and "cardio" to weight training or, as it used to be called, bodybuilding. The stress was now on the muscles. You may think there isn't much to be said on this subject, but in fact there's a whole science of weight training and muscle building, with many controversies and internecine disputes (and even some paradigm shifts). I started reading the bodybuilding magazines, particularly *Flex*, and consulting manuals of muscle development (Arnold

Schwarzenegger has a useful one), learning how to perform the right routines to "build lean muscle". I became, I confess, a bit of a muscle-head (although not, admittedly, a very impressive one).

I want to give my flexing reader a digest of my extensive researches into this field, both theoretically and practically based. I follow the school of bodybuilding founded by the incomparable Mike Mentzer, which advocates three basic principles: *brevity, infrequency, intensity*. This is the exact opposite of what you would naively expect. You might think that to get BIG you need to hit the gym every day and do loads of repetitions as often as you possibly can. But, as Mike points out, this will lead quickly to overtraining and burnout – and worse, small muscles. Look at a marathon runner's legs: thin, right, despite the huge number of repetitions they perform. The key point is that muscles don't grow *while* you stress them; they grow during the recuperation period *after* you stress them. They need to recover from heavy stress, not be continuously subject to it. I'll spare you all the physiological details but the upshot is that the best way to get BIG is to do a few repetitions at high weight no more than once a week per muscle group. Mentzer calls this the *heavy-duty* philosophy. Dorian Yates, the multiple Mr Olympia champion, resident of none other than Birmingham, England, and the most grotesquely muscled man you've ever laid eyes on, subscribes to the heavy-duty philosophy of bodybuilding. Dorian would perform only *one* working set of no more than ten repetitions on each muscle group per week, and this guy is *huge*. His muscles even have muscles. He looks like a mountain range, not a man. He doesn't have an anatomy; he has a geography. How did he get that way? Suppose Dorian is working biceps. He starts with a light warm-up set just to get the blood flowing, nothing too demanding; then he follows that with a ridiculously heavy set of maybe eight repetitions, before leaving biceps alone for a week. That's it: done. Balls to the wall, he engagingly calls it; heavy-duty balls. Now Dorian could lift extremely heavy weights, but for amateurs like you and me the principle is the same: make it intense, very intense, but also brief and infrequent. That way the muscle will be shocked into growing, and it will have enough time to do so – during recuperation – before you shock it again. You send it a message, instead of wearing it down. And the nice thing about this method is that you don't have to spend all your time at the gym. You give it your all for a short period, and then you relax and let nature reap the benefits for you. The secret to getting BIG is *not* overdoing the weight training: quality not quantity.

I followed this extreme muscular philosophy for a while, with decent results, but the method I finally settled into was more of a compromise between Mike and bodybuilding tradition. I'd do three sets per muscle group, about once a week, but sometimes, if I felt strong, I'd do a couple of top-up sets before the week was up. My first set was a warm up: ten reps at medium speed to more-or-less failure. My second set was performed ultra slowly for *six* reps at maximum weight to total failure: this was the "money set". It should be carefully noted here – please pay attention now – that *both* phases of the movement were performed slowly, thereby stressing the muscle to the maximum degree: the weight went up slowly but it also went *down* slowly (this is the killer). For the third set I'd reduce the weight a good bit and then execute it as follows: a quick positive movement up and then a slow negative movement on the way down, also to failure. My philosophy of weight lifting incorporates the notion that muscles respond best when subjected to *variable* stress: some medium, some slow and heavy, some quick combined with slow. One disadvantage of the pure Mike Mentzer method, which Dorian himself eventually fell victim to, is the danger of injury in hitting a muscle so hard so abruptly. The duty can be *too* heavy. On the Colin McGinn method (patent pending), you get the advantage of the super-intense set but you don't put all your eggs in that one basket, with the accompanying risk that you might smash them all. I was about forty years old when I started serious weightlifting and I doubt that my body could handle what younger men can handle. As it was, it would be several days before my muscles had recovered from their ordeal, even after several years of studious lifting. Did I get BIG? Well, I got big-GER. My back, in particular, became a lot thicker and stronger, and I am now a keen advocate of back exercise. The chest is the showy part, but the back is where the body needs its strength. My advice: work on your back, upper and lower.

Was any of this fun? Well, it was more fun than running, mainly because it was over more quickly. Also, you could devise a variety of routines that took away some of the monotony. My weekly schedule proceeded as follows. On Mondays I did chest, shoulders, arms and stomach – bench presses, military presses, flies, biceps curls, crunches and so on. Tuesdays I did nothing (it was one of my teaching days anyway). Wednesday was mainly a back day: first dead lifts for legs and lower back, then cable pull-downs, then seated rows, sometimes pull-ups or kneeling rows with free weights. I'd usually do a bit of arms too, not forgetting triceps – and crunches again. Thursday I took off (more teaching). Friday was a more freewheeling day, a mixed salad of exercises, with maybe some squats and leg extensions. Weekends were off. It doesn't sound like much, but it was enough; if I did more I'd start to feel over-trained and it would be a grind to be in the gym. Following this regime for over ten years put me in pretty decent shape, I'm happy to report. Nor did I suffer any injuries. I'd recommend weight training for anyone, especially when you get older, when muscle mass is apt to diminish: but the thing is, *it isn't sport*. It's exercise. Beyond minimal coordination it requires no real skill, just the necessary will power and some enlightened masochism. Most serious athletes today do weight training (just look, for example, at Rafael Nadal's biceps) and performance has improved as a consequence; but weight training isn't really a sport in itself, despite sporadic efforts to get it accepted as an Olympic event. It's good for fitness, sure, and vanity, obviously, but it lacks the rewards of sport proper.

Bodybuilding brings up the issue of drugs, specifically steroids. It's an open secret that all professional bodybuilders use steroids. Why? Because they manifestly work; just look at the difference between so-called natural bodybuilders and the monsters that use steroids. No comparison; no contest. Obviously, too, drugs boost performance in cycling, running and baseball, and no doubt any other sport that requires muscular power. That's why athletes take them. Have I been tempted to use steroids? Well, I have used legal nutritional supplements, as well as Creatine, a chemical that helps muscles process energy. I probably would have used steroids if they had been legal: at least I'd have given it a try to see what the results were. You may be shocked: aren't performance-enhancing drugs dangerous, and unethical, and the Beginning of the End? Don't we want our bodies to improve by "natural" means and not with the aid of artificial stimulants? Isn't it unfair to your competitors in a sport to exploit the unnatural advantage conferred by steroids and their ilk? Aren't drugs the very antithesis of the essential spirit of sport? These are questions one hears often enough, and they are generally taken to show that drugs are a cheat, a fraud, an injustice, a health hazard and whatnot. But actually things aren't really so clear-cut: it's quite hard to defend any of this anti-drug rhetoric on rational grounds – independently of the hysteria that regularly surrounds the word *drug*. Let me briefly assess the various arguments against using drugs in sport, either competitively or in the privacy of your own basement. The issue is large and controversial, but I want to suggest caution in condemning the use of drugs in sport; the issue is more nuanced than is generally recognized.

First, the dangers: are performance-enhancing drugs bad for your health? Well, they are in large and irresponsible quantities; but then so is aspirin or even running up stairs. Apparently, however, there is no real evidence to suggest that moderate regulated use is much of a health hazard; or if it is, it isn't any worse than health hazards regularly courted by athletes – boxers and football players being the obvious examples, but also gymnasts, divers and hockey players. Most sports have their dangers, but few people would like to criminalize them on that account; and it is generally felt that the benefits outweigh the dangers. Diets have their risks too, but does anyone think dieting is an unacceptable way to enhance sporting ability? And what is this notion of "natural" that is being invoked? Most of the training techniques, and dietary regimes, used by athletes are not "natural" in any clear sense; and besides, steroids are in fact a natural ingredient of the human body (if you have low steroid levels, doctors will prescribe steroid supplements). Is it unfair to use steroids to gain a competitive edge? But athletes use all sorts of things to gain a competitive edge, including their own innate endowment, superior training facilities, better coaches, superior diet. (In the old days, it was deemed unethical to use a coach or even to train before an event – a gentleman should just be able to go out there and do it without any effort or preparation.) Besides, athletes could all choose to use this extra training measure to improve their performance, if it were legal; it's not that only some would be *allowed* to use drugs and not others. Why aren't steroids, properly administered, just one more way we have discovered to enhance physical performance? Even if they lead in some cases to long-term health problems, this doesn't set them apart from other aspects of athletic activity. A good case can be made that they should be decriminalized, regulated and employed responsibly (not given to children, for example). Given that some athletes will use them anyway, it levels the playing field to make them freely available. The situation we have now, in which some people illegally use drugs to gain an edge, certainly seems no better than one in which things are more open. The case is analogous to the issue of drug legalization in general: a good case can be made that most of the problems stem from illegality itself, not from the drugs considered in themselves. Prohibition doesn't work, and it's not clear by what rational criterion some substances are banned and not others.

Much more can be said, and has been said, on this subject (and see the Further Reading), but I hope I've said enough to give you a taste of the reasons to be sceptical of the usual reflex hostility to drug use in sport. I'd be in favour of legalizing all such performance-enhancing substances, with proper safeguards applied, and letting individuals decide whether they want to avail themselves of their proven powers. (I have the same view of so-called recreational drugs such as marijuana: like tobacco and alcohol, they should be legal but regulated.) I rather resent not being given the choice as to whether to use steroids as a bodybuilding aid. It's my body, after all – shouldn't I have the right to do what I want with it? The issue is an example of an important political controversy – between paternalism and libertarianism. Paternalism permits the state to interfere with the choices of individual citizens if it deems that interference to be in the best interests of the individual, as with seatbelt and crash-helmet laws. Libertarianism holds that individuals should be free to act as they desire so long as their actions do no harm to others, even when those actions may harm themselves. We are clearly all paternalists when it comes to children, but many have felt that paternalism goes too far when it prohibits intelligent voting adults from exercising their freedom of choice in regard purely to their own welfare. Drugs are an obvious test case: shouldn't it be up to me whether I take steroids to improve my muscularity, even if it might cause me harm – just as smoking and drinking are up to me under our current laws? In fact, it's not clear that it will cause me significant harm, but so what if it does? The problem with the paternalist argument against drugs is that there are all sorts of things the state allows me to do that far more clearly entail personal risk: drive a car, have unprotected sex, eat bad food. Why ban steroids but not ban unhealthy food? Some people will no doubt abuse both, but that is their problem, and why should their poor judgement prevent me from exercising my better judgement? Suppose that as I grow older my body won't allow me, because of muscular atrophy, to engage in the athletic activities that help give my life meaning, but that a few steroid pills a week will restore me to vigour and stamina, with minimal risk of side effects (and which *legal* drugs have no side effects?). I would be extremely annoyed if the state legally bans me from taking those steroids, consigning me to frustration and misery. I should prefer to adopt the libertarian view of the matter, leaving it up to individuals whether to enhance their performance with steroids. What I would insist on is that such use be transparent, so that all athletes know who is taking what. And if a substantial proportion of them don't wish to use steroids, I would suggest forming a different league for the drug-using and drug-free athletes, assuming the drugs make a really dramatic difference to performance; rather as women don't normally compete with men and boxers are assigned to different weight classes. In my judgement, the current hysteria about performance-enhancing drugs is part of a larger hysteria about drugs that cannot withstand rational scrutiny. But to go into that broader question would take me too far afield. I shall therefore leave the matter here, conscious that my position will strike some people as irresponsible – and others as simple common sense. My main concern in this book is with the rewards of sport to the individual, not the social and legal aspects of professional sports.

Let's leave the sweaty precincts of the gym and breathe in the mountain air for a while. I had never been on skis until I was forty-seven years old. Growing up in England in the 1950s and 1960s, no one seemed to ski – no one I knew anyway; you'd have to go abroad, to start with, and it would be expensive. But I decided, relatively late in life, before it was too late, that I wanted to give it a try. So I went out and bought some ski equipment, *before* I ever went skiing – that's how committed I was. Not just the jacket, pants, goggles and so on, but also the skis, boots and poles. Thus equipped, I drove up to Hunter Mountain, two hours from New York City, with Cathy, who had been skiing since high school (and who later became my third wife). She was to be my patient ski instructor, although I had prepared myself by watching a skiing video, booted on my new skis in the living room at home. I was *set*. Soon I'd be merrily skiing away. How hard could it be? You stand on the skis and go downhill, right? Nothing to it. I had images of myself tearing down the slopes, carefree and controlled, all whizz and zip.

Carrying the skis proved to be a serious challenge. Getting them on in snow was a major ordeal. Staying upright on them for longer than a second was virtually impossible. I fell several times just getting into the bindings; and once I was in and attached to the skis, they simply started to move of their own accord, one leg bidding a fond farewell to the other. My first run on the "nursery slope", with the rather more confident and contained three-year-olds, saw me crouched forward, poles clutched tight, accelerating downhill, utterly out of control, until I lost balance and wiped out. My second run was the same. And so was my third. I had to learn how to *turn* – to retard the acceleration by applying pressure to the downward ski, thus skiing across the fall line, not straight down it. The trouble was, every time I applied the requisite pressure I fell over. After an hour or so of this nonsense, I seriously thought I had met my match: I was never going to learn how to ski, just not cut out for it, not in my genes. Anyone reading this now who learned how to ski as a grown-up will recognize my description: it's *so* much harder than it looks. But I persisted, progressing through the early phase of the snowplough formation of the skis, until I could ski with them more or less in parallel and not crouching ignominiously forward all the time. That took a couple of years, though, and quite a lot of money. Cathy was patient, dawdling with me on the beginner slopes, waiting for me to catch up with her. I had my humiliating tangles with bushes at the side of the run; I attempted intermediate slopes that left me gasping and swearing; I even toppled over as I dismounted from the chairlift once or twice. In addition, my instinctive fear of heights was at its most intense on the chair lifts whenever they were more than ten feet from the ground, which is to say, most of the time (maybe I should have mentioned this to Cathy before we set out). It's also incredibly hard on the legs, especially when your skill level is low: the constant pressure you have to exert to keep from getting out of control makes your quadriceps feel like rubber after a couple of hours. The following morning, waking up to face yet another tough day on the mountain, your legs start protesting as soon as you stand up ("Surely you aren't suggesting that we go through that again!"). It's not all relaxed gliding and après-ski frolicking. It's *hard*.

And yet, I couldn't wait to get out there again. The natural beauty is a large part of it. I started travelling to Utah and Colorado to ski, with the big mountains, and the big sky, and the perfect snow. The views alone are worth the (steep) price of lift passes. But it's the total experience of skiing down a massive mountain, in the clear crisp air, with the blue sky and the infinite distance, and the acres of inviting white, that makes it so enjoyable. And you do learn to ski better all the time, with less pain and more style. For anyone considering taking it up, the essential point to note is that it's possible to have a great time skiing and not be very good at it. I know. Once you can stay upright and control your speed, you are ready to enjoy the experience. When the fear recedes and your legs stop hurting, you can gaze around happily and carve your way down to the bottom in perfect bliss. Even now, several years later, I'm still a pretty feeble skier, unable to take on advanced slopes, and often overtaken by eight-year-olds and old ladies, but I have a fine old time out there. I flatter myself that I don't look too ungainly any more, and might even be mistaken for a decent skier who is taking it easy for a change. But I'm definitely at the lower end of the skill spectrum. I watch the beginners, though, crouching forward, clutching the poles, making with the snowplough, toppling over, and I think, well, at least I'm not *that* bad any more. The simple fact is that I should have started sooner. I should really have been born in Switzerland, come to think of it.

Skiing illustrates nicely the aesthetic dimension to sports. You can't help noticing the difference between a clumsy, ugly skier and a graceful, beautiful skier. Good technique is invariably beautiful technique. You *feel* ugly when you start out in that ungainly crouch, skidding and flailing. Increase of skill is experienced as aesthetic enhancement. Form and performance go together. This is why people like to wear attractive ski clothes: because the whole exercise is an aesthetic one. The mountain is beautiful, as is the activity, so you may as well look lovely too (I myself have a really spiffy ski jacket). The experience of skiing is a strongly aesthetic experience, at least when you can do it properly. Some romantics have conjectured that sports *are* an art form, akin to dance, to be assessed accordingly. That seems to me to be going too far: just because an activity has an aesthetic dimension doesn't make it an art form (is surgery an art form?). But I do think that part of the attraction of sport – and some sports more than others – is an aesthetic attraction. This is obvious for diving, figure-skating and gymnastics, but even a well-executed pass in football (in either the English or American sense) has its elegance and flair. We derive specifically aesthetic pleasure from watching sport and from doing it. It's hard to think of any sport that doesn't appeal to the senses in this way. Even the shot put has its grace and arc.

Then too, there is the aesthetic quality of the equipment. I admit it: I'm an equipment freak. As soon as I acquired the basic skills, I had to buy new skis and poles (although I still use my first boots). Good equipment makes all the difference in skiing, I maintain; even the goggles have to be just-so. But any kind of sporting equipment entrances me. There is nature, and there is the human body; but without the right equipment to mediate between the two nothing much can happen. Whoever invented skis must have been thrilled with this new way of mediating body and nature. A sport like skiing involves a nexus of person, nature and equipment; they all work together as a unified whole. The moment when the skis stop feeling like an encumbrance and become an extension of your body is when everything is working as a unity. People can become extremely attached to their equipment, emotionally, and lavish great care on its maintenance; and that is nothing to be surprised at, given that equipment and body become fused in the activity in question. Pleasure in one's equipment is part of the attraction of sport, a theme I'll come back to. (Don't men refer to a certain precious part of their body as their "equipment"?)

I learned to ice skate as a teenager in Blackpool, in the local rink. The object of the exercise then was to tear nonchalantly round the rink at top speed, whooshing past groups of slow-moving girls. I had the fearlessness of youth back then and could tolerate the odd spill or bump (the local heavies were more of a danger). I started skating again in Manhattan, usually at the Wollman Rink in Central Park, sometimes at the Sky Rink at Chelsea Piers. (I'd also taken up rollerblading, which I used to do around the Loop in Central Park, along with all the other show-offs and misfits.) I now had much better ice skates than I did as a boy, the hockey type, but I skated far more cautiously, sensibly enough in the circumstances. The essence of the skill is placing your full weight on one skate at a time, so that you are basically balancing on one leg. I could do it well enough, but longed for a greater sense of freedom and confidence. This led to my first experience with the game of ice hockey. In the Connecticut winters, I used to skate with my nephews and nieces on a frozen pond in their back yard, and the two boys, Connor and Griffyn, played hockey at school. I *had* to give it a try, after watching them slam the puck, imprudent as that may appear. My first effort resulted in a banged head and a bruised rear. It's one thing to skate smoothly in a straight line, obeying Newton's first law of motion, but in hockey it's all turning, twisting and sudden acceleration. After a couple of injuries I realized I needed the proper protective equipment, and that was no hard-sell for the equipment freak I have confessed myself to be. So I acquired the whole package:

my own hockey stick, obviously, a helmet with visor, pads for the knees and elbows, those special hockey gloves with the big fingers, and the thickly padded shorts for cushioning the pelvis when you crash into the ice – plus the optional socks and jersey. I looked the part – before you saw me take to the ice, that is. Thus cushioned, my proneness to injury was minimized (although I did manage to sprain my ankle quite badly). I could now skate and hustle, swivel and halt, without the old anxiety about hitting the ice. The fun of whacking the puck fast across the ice, into the goal, while moving at speed, was worth all the effort (and expense). How skilful did I get? Well, when ten-year-old Griffyn skated straight towards me – fast, agile, merciless – I stood absolutely no chance: I could only lunge and totter as he flashed by towards the goal. My only consolation is that he went on to become the star of his local team and now, at fourteen years old, tours the country in junior hockey matches. I envy him and wish I'd had those opportunities as a youngster; but at least I've had a taste of the experience he clearly relishes. The general lesson for my sport-shy reader is that even a sport as demanding as ice hockey is something you can attempt at almost any age, given the opportunity; I guarantee you will learn a lot. And the equipment is something else.

I don't think I can avoid the issue of age and death. I have to come clean about my attitude to this diabolical partnership. You might have thought that the reward for enduring old age would be rebirth, not extinction. There you are, after stoically staying the course, as your body has withered and sagged, a mere shadow of your former self, and instead of being born again you are summarily put to death! That can't be right, can it? Who came up with that arrangement? Age followed quickly by death: a major double whammy there. (What if we were born old and gradually got younger as the years went by, eventually reaching infancy and finally non-existence? That seems a lot easier to take. Just think of how much you would look forward to your twenties!) As I grow older, I find that my enthusiasm for sport increases, instead of diminishing. I'd rather develop a good backhand than churn out another book. As I observed in Chapter 2, it was at its nadir in my twenties (I would never have written a book like this back then). Now I no longer "have my whole life ahead of me" – no, not even half of it. I can't procrastinate and postpone, telling myself I'll get round to it one day. I can't let my academic work take the front seat every time. I want to learn and practise these skills while I'm still young and fit enough to do so (I'm fifty-seven now – unbelievably, to me anyway). Also, I want to *stay* young; physical deterioration alarms and depresses me. Doing sports helps with this, of course: it staves off the effects of age. Presumably, most people share my mortal concerns. No one wants to age and die. To them I say, "Do it!" I learned to ski and play ice hockey relatively late in life, among other activities not yet mentioned, and if I can do it so can you (remember, I'm a desk-bound philosopher by profession). It helps me cope with aging, and in a wholly positive way.

But do I perhaps nurture a superstitious attitude toward sport? Do I somehow think that it will magically buy me immortality? How *can* I grow old and die when I can still do all these things? Of course, I know that is nonsense – intellectually. Age will come, death will follow hard on its heels. I'll slow down. I'll lose my timing, my strength, even my desire. It *will* happen. But do I in some pocket of my being not really believe this? Do I harbour the hope that sport will keep me going strong for ever? And, you know, to be honest, I think I *do* believe that. Sport is my answer to mortality; it's what my will to live incites me to believe. It is what I fling at mortality to keep it at bay. Sport is my refusal to die. And even when I do become incapacitated by age, and near death, I will look back at my athletic endeavours as my protest against finitude. I just wasn't going to take it lying down. The lesson I draw from this is that sport is especially suitable for the middle aged. It keeps depression at bay, as well as actual deterioration. So long as you are acquiring new physical skills you are keeping your body alive – not just ticking but throbbing. I have a friend (George S.) who is seventy-seven years old and he plays tennis doubles several times a week. He can't move very quickly around the court any more, but he is a sharp and skilful player, and life burns within him during a match. If I can keep going until I'm that age I'll be happy. With sport eighty is the new forty. Death will come sure enough, but we don't have to let it slow us down – not just yet anyway.

I need to get you up to speed on my own tennis life (and I can't bear to end the chapter on such a gloomy note). You will recall that I used to play with Andrew in wet and blustery Blackpool as a teenager but that I stopped playing for many years. I started playing again with my publisher, Robert, in New York in the mid-1990s, in Central Park. We played once a week for a few months. I never took a lesson, however. My game did improve marginally, although I was still an inept player, enamoured of the defensive forehand slice and the desperate drop shot. I hit the ball out whenever I tried to give it some pace. My serve was either a limp lob or a hopelessly ambitious smash. I tried to play tennis with the same set of skills I employed in table tennis, which is not a good way to play (too much wrist). But those inferior efforts gave me a renewed taste for the game and a desire to one day become *good*. I could see my faults, although I didn't know what to do about them, yet I also felt I had potential. The experience started me on my ongoing quest to play tennis *properly*. I wasn't going to quit this earth never having learned how to hit a tennis ball correctly. There are some things in life that simply have to be done.

4. Into the water

It all started with a humble piece of Styrofoam, four feet by three – a great watershed, so to speak, in my life. That was the seed, the singularity. My son Bruno (now a fully grown doctor) was visiting me in the US – he was fifteen at the time – and we decided to take a road trip to Florida from New York, a good eighteen hour journey. He lived in Cornwall then and was a keen body-boarder, equipped with wetsuit, fins – the works. He suggested we rent a board, also called a "boogie board", for amusement at the beach. We checked out Ron Jon's in Cocoa Beach, a huge surfing shop (I'd never been into one before), and found that the boogie boards were on sale, so I bought one with a dark green bottom and grey plastic top for about sixty bucks. It wasn't top of the line, but it was serviceable enough, and it was only going to see a couple of weeks of use. Little did I know what would grow from that initial germ!

I had always regarded the beach with some misgivings. I'd walk on it in Blackpool with the dog, but I had no great interest in lingering there. On summer holidays to Greece or Spain I'd dutifully acquire a bit of a tan, but found myself generally bored on the sand. I didn't much like to read on the beach, because of the glare of the sun, and after an hour or so I was just too hot and bothered. I'd go in the water for a dip and a perfunctory swim, but that palled quickly too. I was constitutionally beach-averse; I didn't even like the sand clinging between my toes. The boogie board at least offered the prospect of something to *do* there, instead of just lying around baking. When Bruno took the board out I watched him from afar, and he was soon catching modest waves (and complaining he didn't have his fins with him). I thought I may as well have a go myself, but had no high expectations. It turned out to be a lot more difficult than it looked (isn't everything?). You have to leash the board to your wrist, lie on top of it, grip it with one hand, and then paddle out through the waves with your other hand. The board kept slipping out from under me and it was tough to make progress through the waves. If a big wave came, I got knocked off my precarious perch. The water kept hitting me full in the face, stinging my eyes. By the time I made it out to the breaking waves, I was exhausted. And then I had to catch a ride. This required a vigorous paddling action with my free hand, while keeping the board in position in the tumult. I failed several times, merely tumbling over or losing my grip on the board. This surfing lark, not what it's cracked up to be. But after a short while, a nice clean wave approached, mounting, curling, peaking; I paddled in front of it, and actually caught the thing. It carried me forward for about ten metres. That moment changed my life, literally. I was forty-four years of age, and heretofore a confirmed landlubber. *I like that*, I thought. So I did it a few more times, until I was too tired to continue. I had surfed for the first time. Nothing spectacular, you understand, but a wave had been caught and ridden. Now I knew what to do at the beach; now there was a point to being there. Sometimes your own children can be quite educational, can't they?

Returning to New York, I was set on continuing my new pastime. Bruno persuaded me to buy a wetsuit for use in the colder waters up north, and to equip myself with proper fins for gaining acceleration at the take-off point. Then I also needed a special bag to carry the board in, along with other bits and pieces. You don't need to work very hard to get me to buy sporting equipment, and besides, it really wasn't that expensive. I started travelling out to the beaches of Long Island, mainly at Jones Beach, so as to continue my new passion for the water. I think what most appealed to me about it was floating on the water, instead of being submerged in it; no more struggling to keep my mouth and nose water-free, but maintaining a safe distance – on, but not in, the stuff. On a board, it feels like the water is bearing you up rather than sucking you down. Another man I knew, Michael, whom I sometimes played tennis with, also got into it, equipping himself with the gear, and we went out to the beach together. We were two middle-aged beginner boogie boarders, one bald and the other less so, no doubt averting our pair of midlife crises. You would have to smile – especially watching these two characters trying to walk in those flippers. One day I saw a lifeguard in a kayak, paddling near the shore, and as a wave came he caught it, surfing in smoothly. For some reason, the idea immediately appealed to me, and I boldly asked if I could give it a try, not that I'd ever been in a kayak before. A wave appeared and pushed me forwards for a few seconds; I wouldn't go so far as to claim that I actually *surfed* the thing. But I felt the force of the wave as it set the boat in motion, firm but yielding, and could appreciate the potential. Also, I liked the feel of the paddle in my hands, with the possibilities of manoeuvrability it conferred. The feel of a sport is its primal attraction, its way into the sensory-motor brain. The kayak was a short plastic sit-on-top, nothing very fancy, but it gave me ideas. Kayaking suddenly seemed the way to go. In that moment I felt born to kayak.

Back in Manhattan, I decided I needed a kayak of my very own; or my sensory-motor brain decided that (it has its own cravings). After researching the matter, I ended up buying a twelve foot foldable kayak made by Feathercraft of Canada: a bright red K1 to be precise, costing about $1000, not cheap by any means. It needed to be the folding kind because I planned to keep it in my apartment, on the ninth floor. And where was I intending to paddle my spanking new boat? In the Hudson River, naturally, a block away from my house. What objection could there be to that? (I used to run beside it; now I'd kayak on it.) As it turned out, setting the thing up was no easy feat, involving much swearing and soreness of the fingers; it took me about four hours all told, instead of the twenty minutes it was supposed to take, once you knew how to do it. It squatted there in my living room, athwart the sofa, splendid in its red and black (the cat peed in the cockpit when I was out, which didn't please me). It became evident to me, however, that I'd need to store it nearer the water, because folding it up and reassembling it were not the work of a moment, and carrying it over there erect wasn't feasible. (Are kayaks phallic? Neither more nor less than most sporting equipment; consider for a moment the pole-vaulting pole: *ouch*.) As it happens, there was a marina of sorts at 89th Street, five minutes walk from my apartment, and the city of New York allows people, for a modest fee, to store kayaks in a large underground garage there, gloomy and grimy though it be. So I installed my new K1 in the designated kayak cage, eager to begin my new kayaking life: eager to become a *kayaker*. Who would have thought that the Upper West Side of Manhattan would be a kayak haven?

The first time I put it in the brownish water of the Hudson (sadly dirtying it up) I forgot to put the "sea sock" into the cockpit area and I hadn't thought to install flotation bags inside either; so when I predictably capsized into the river near the dock, the boat filled with water and nearly sank. That was harrowing; I quickly realized the perils, to man and machine. From then on I took all precautions, including always wearing a life vest, and making sure the boat wouldn't sink if it capsized again. In fact, I never did capsize again in the river, although I was always in fear of it because of the difficulty of getting back in the boat again. Soon I was crossing the river to the New Jersey side, negotiating large vessels, paddling up as far as the George Washington bridge, and generally having a good kayaking time. I felt … adventurous. My friend Michael, not one to be left out (or outdone), decided he needed to become a kayaker too, so he bought the next model up from mine from Feathercraft, along with many gadgets and accessories, including a marine radio. We used to venture out there together, summer and winter, paddling the dark and turbid waters of the Hudson. It became an obsession. I particularly liked tucking myself into the "spray skirt" that kept water from seeping into the cockpit; I felt snug and protected. We were the object of many an appreciative stare from landlocked would-be kayak adventurers, as well as the odd "Are you guys nuts?"

One thing I cottoned on to early was the importance of tides. The Hudson has strong tidal currents, reaching a good four knots at the height of the ebb or flow. Before I properly appreciated this, I went out one day and made tremendous progress paddling north, going for about twenty minutes. I could tell I was receiving some assistance from the tide, but underestimated how much. When I turned to come back I was making *zero* progress: I had to paddle hard to stay in one place and as soon as I stopped paddling I travelled backwards. Since you can't easily get out of the river in the Manhattan area – it's mostly bordered by high concrete walls – I was stuck where I was and had to hang on to some rocks until the tide changed. (Moral: *don't* go with the flow.) From then on I consulted the tide charts, making a point of timing my trips so that I had the tide with me in both directions. However, that was not so easy to arrange, as the tide waits for no man, and I'd have to be careful never to travel too far in the direction of the flow. This is a sport in which nature calls the shots. As the ancient kayaker said, you've got to respect the water.

I took a lesson in kayaking technique, which I'd recommend to anyone thinking of taking up the sport. I've now repeated this lesson dozens of times to novice paddlers; so stand by for some useful information. First, grip the paddle with both hands at shoulder width, with the sharper side of the paddle blade pointing up. Note that most paddles have the blades set at an angle to each other (they are "feathered"), so that the wind doesn't catch the blades too much as you paddle. This means that you have to rotate the paddle shaft through enough of an angle to allow the blade to enter cleanly and effectively into the water (to achieve the proper "catch"). To bring that about you grip the paddle in your right hand (assuming you're right-handed), firmly but not too tightly, and then rotate it as needed through the loose fingers of your left hand as you dip the paddle from side to side. Neither hand should make a full fist; the first few fingers are generally enough for a proper grip. (Here, let me show you.) You need to relax the fingers if you're going to paddle a long distance. Now – and this is important – plant the blade into the water fairly far forwards, near your feet if possible, and draw it back in a long slow movement, fully submerging the blade, so that you get a good strong catch. Don't just dip it in and pull it back a few inches before switching to the other side. You shouldn't be powering the paddle with your arms alone, using primarily your biceps muscle; this will tire you out very quickly. Instead, you must keep your arms more or less straight during the stroke and use your upper body to twist and generate power. This – the "torso twist" – enables you to use the bigger muscles of your upper body to generate momentum, not the smaller muscles of the arms. The snag is that moving your body in this way generates instability, so that novice paddlers strive to keep their torso perfectly still and move their arms exclusively. But you should know that once the paddle blade is firmly in the water and being pulled through it, you acquire a lot of stability thereby; the paddle acts like an outrigger that gives you another point of balance. You are most unstable in a kayak when you first get in and don't yet have the paddle in the water. Once you are moving, you acquire enough stability to execute the torso twist quite safely. You will find that you move forwards with far greater power and you can paddle all day; plus it looks a lot better. There is an art to the paddle stroke – and I've only covered the basics here – and it takes a decent amount of practice to master it. Most recreational paddlers you see out there don't do it properly at all: stiff body, bent arms, too firm a grip, truncated catch.

They don't have the requisite know-how, and they don't know they don't know. Once you have mastered the stroke, there is much you know that you didn't know before. You have become, in a sense, better educated, with your body the repository of knowledge. And you glide forwards with effortless grace. There is epistemic and aesthetic enhancement in learning to paddle properly.

Now that I had a storage place for my K1, I didn't need to worry about having a foldable boat. I quickly discovered that my twelve foot kayak – although a nice beginner boat – was not designed for speed, and that a longer fibreglass boat would be much swifter in the water. So I purchased a nineteen foot Kevlar sea kayak from Seda of California, the aptly named Glider, and had it shipped out to New York. It was white with a teal deck, a very spiffy vessel, lacquered and long. I well remember the first time I tried that boat out in the Hudson: it was a cold, misty and windless morning – and the boat glided silently, smoothly and rapidly through the water, fully living up to its name. Money well spent, I thought (and I'm not even going to tell you what it cost). In it I looked like the seasoned and global kayaker I wasn't. I lost count of the number of people who asked me what "a thing like that" cost, and the stunned look on their faces when I told them the figure. But it had one not inconsiderable drawback: you couldn't turn the thing around in anything stronger than a light breeze. As soon as you turned the boat so that the wind was hitting it directly broadside, it wouldn't turn any further. Its ample surface area and length caught the wind in such a way that you couldn't generate enough force with the paddle for the boat to complete the last part of its turn. It just stuck there, pinned by the wind. This meant that the only way you could go back to where you started was to get out of the boat on dry land and turn it round by hand, which obviously isn't always feasible. So I couldn't go out in it if the wind was at all strong, and would find myself in trouble if it picked up while I was out. Yes, it would glide fast and easy in a straight line, but you couldn't turn the damn thing around!

This is an instance of a general truth about kayaks: their upsides always have a downside, mathematically so. What's good for one job won't do for another. The better they track the worse they turn and vice versa.

Anyway, that didn't stop me from car-topping the Glider down to North Carolina one summer, along with my old K1. I was hoping to try surf kayaking again, as well as do some flat water paddling. Everything went according to plan, except that neither boat was remotely suitable for surfing. That was clear for the long boat, but the shorter boat had the problem that whenever I capsized in it – which was often – it would fill with water and needed to be taken to the beach and emptied out. It became extremely heavy when full of water and therefore difficult to handle, and also lethal if a wave crashed it into you as you were trying to get it on to the beach. But I did catch my first waves in that unsuitable vehicle, which made me determined to persist. One thing that happened distressingly often was that when I caught a wave the boat would "pearl", that is, take a nose dive down the face of the wave. This meant that I went with it, lodged inside the cockpit of the boat, sometimes being turned upside down by the wave. From that alarming position I had to exit the boat and swim to the surface: always a tense few seconds. Then I had to swim the thing to shore, empty it and try again. However, this exigent routine was eventually terminated by my pearling too near the beach and driving the nose into the sand, thus buckling the aluminium frame of the boat. Basically, I wrecked it. Sorry, K1. I had fun doing so, though – incompetent fun, but fun.

I realized I needed a specially designed surf kayak, so I exchanged my damaged K1 for a Piranha Surfjet. This was made of rotomoulded plastic, and was about nine feet long, and wide, with a flat bottom and a sit-on-top, which meant that it didn't hold water when it capsized. I also exchanged my Glider, reluctantly, for a sixteen foot Dagger Meridian that *did* turn in the wind: more rocker, shorter, less surface area. With the new surf kayak, I started riding the waves off the Jersey shore and sometimes in Long Island – not very expertly, admittedly, but at least I was finally catching waves without suffering my earlier problems. The Meridian I used mainly in the Hudson, and very satisfactory it was, with its storage compartments and deck webbing. So after a couple of false starts and some equipment issues, I was now getting somewhere in the kayaking sphere. The main trouble was, now that I was doing it better, I wanted to do it more, and the opportunities were few and far between. Living in Manhattan, it's not so easy to get your surfing in. No decent waves on Broadway.

I haven't said much, if anything, about *why* I took to surfing. What did I get out of it? It was a major hassle to get to the beach, what with all the car-topping and equipment-lugging; and my time in the water could be wearisome and frustrating, waiting for waves that never came or being buffeted by recalcitrant ones. So what was the appeal? What *is* it about surfing? The problem here is that it's hard to put it into words. I can tell you that it's a thrill to feel the wave start to pick you up and then to ride down it, but that seems rather lame and unconvincing. Philosophers sometimes talk about knowledge you can have only by experiencing something: "knowledge by acquaintance". For example, you can't know what red is like without actually experiencing red, or what an orgasm is like without having one yourself. By contrast, you can know that Paris is the capital of France without directly experiencing Paris or France, or that Darwin's theory of evolution is true without directly experiencing evolution (this is sometimes called "knowledge by description"). Well, surfing is like redness and orgasm: you can't know what it's like without experiencing it yourself. You can get an *idea* by comparing it to other experiences you've had, such as sliding down an inclined plane or being carried on someone's shoulders, but you can't grasp the whole thing without actually doing it yourself. It's much the same with other sports, and surely this is part of their appeal: they provide types of experience that are not available

67

by other means, and these experiences are felt to be valuable. The thing about surfing, though, is that it's rather *unlike* experiences you would have in the normal run of events (not like surfing the internet, say). When you learn how to surf, you come to have two kinds of knowledge: knowledge of how to perform the activity ("practical knowledge") and knowledge of what it *feels like* to perform the activity ("phenomenological knowledge"). In general, knowledge of a sporting skill has these two components: practical knowledge and phenomenological knowledge. Neither type of knowledge can be fully conveyed by mere description, just by *telling* someone what you know about the sport. You have to *do* it, and *feel* what it's like to do it. The thing that cannot be conveyed by words alone is simply the *experience of doing it*: the phenomenology of a skill. Sometimes I teach people how to surf kayak and there is always that moment when they first catch a wave and their eyes say, "*Now* I see why people like to do this!" A new piece of knowledge has been pumped into their heads; all the words in the world couldn't put it in there before. Of course, the incommunicability of such knowledge is somewhat of a handicap when writing a *book* about sport, because the author is trying to use words to capture something that is really only available through practical experience. Each sport has its characteristic phenomenology – what it's like to engage in it – and without direct experience you can have only a vague idea of what that phenomenology is all about. Learning a sport is expanding the range of your experience, coming to know more about what human beings can sense and feel – and surely this is part of why we value it. Sport is ancient and universal across cultures, and that must be because the experiences it affords are deemed valuable by participants, and are specific to sport. The experiences characteristic of sport cannot be obtained by any means *other* than sport. The point I'm making now is that this value is not appreciable without direct acquaintance; it can't be learned from books or lectures alone, however dithyrambic the rhetoric may be. In other words, to put it bluntly, the essence of sport is ineffable. This is why I have not indulged in florid descriptions of the joys of surfing: I recognize that all such descriptions will fall short of the mark. Better to acknowledge that direct experience is indispensable here. People who have shared this type of experience can talk to each other meaningfully about it, but an outsider to the activity is also an outsider to the meaning of talk about it. So those who have no interest in sport and have never engaged in it, even rudimentarily, are unlikely to understand why those who love it feel the way they do. It's like the blind not knowing what the fuss about seeing colours is all about, or the pre-orgasmic child wondering why adults seem so obsessed with this mysterious thing called "sex". I don't mean to criticize either party; my point is an epistemological one – you can't know what participating in a sport like surfing is all about without doing it yourself. Ride a wave and then come back to me, in short.

Part of my aim in describing my own experience with particular sports, dwelling on their physical details, as well as their trials, is that I want to convey as much as I can about the feel of sport, and not merely lapse into windy generalities and strained analogies (it's like sex, mystical experience, disco dancing, whatever). Sport is like sport – as pole vaulting is like … pole vaulting. I can tell you that surfing involves the pleasures of the ocean and the open air, and the thrill of coordinated control over body and nature: all true, but that doesn't at all add up to what it's *really* like. To know that you've got to get out into the water with your surf board or boat, practice, struggle, swear and gasp, until one day you're sliding down a wave feeling happy to be alive. In fact, I won't even try to say more about the phenomenology of surfing, because I'll only misrepresent it. (Do surfers adopt in-words such as "gnarly" precisely because of the ineffability of their sport?) I will say that when you see the wave approaching, you have to paddle hard (I'm speaking of surf kayaking now), lean forwards, orient the boat along the line of the wave (not straight down – that will make you pearl), and then use your weight and the paddle to guide you along the wave, up to the crest, down to the trough, until the wave peters out and you can dismount from it, ready to paddle out again for the next one. I will also say, mysteriously I hope, that the wave becomes *yours*.

Now I must broach a delicate issue, around which emotions can run strong. Board surfers reading the above may feel a sense of resentment, since I have neglected their worthy sport in favour of surf kayaking. And the truth is I'm a pretty dismal board surfer. Sure, I have a couple of long boards, and I've been to Hawaii to learn how to surf, but I don't do it much and am not too hot at it. But I'm not disrespecting it: nothing could be further from my thoughts. I'd love to be an expert (or even competent) stand-up surfer (and will keep working at it when the occasion arises), but in fact I'm most comfortable in a kayak and that's the way I learned to surf. I prefer being able to sit upright with a paddle to power me forwards, instead of lying face down on the board using only my hands to move through the water, waves hitting me in the face and all that good stuff; and I find it a lot easier to stay seated, using the paddle and my weight to guide my movements. Maybe stand-up surfing is the purer form – it certainly strikes me as harder to do – but I think I am within my rights to describe what I do in a kayak as surfing, possibly of a debased and dubious kind. In fact, I've never encountered any hostility from board surfers, even though in a kayak I can catch waves earlier than they can, in virtue of the greater volume of the platform. Anyway, what I said above about the joys of surf kayaking carries over, *mutatis mutandis*, to regular surfing. So, we're cool, right?

As noted earlier, my problem was that I didn't have sufficient opportunity to pursue my new passion. Living in Manhattan, I'd have to drive out to a coastal area at weekends or go on a summer holiday for a couple of weeks and hope for waves. And the Hudson River isn't, let's face it, the ideal place to kayak at the best of times – crowded with boats, dirty, tidal, none too scenic. So I came up with the obvious plan: buy a house on Long Island, near the ocean, which I could live in during the summers (Manhattan is hellishly hot in the summer anyway), and from which I could pursue my aquatic enthusiasms. I happened to meet a fellow Englishman, Danny, originally from Yorkshire but a Long Island resident for some twenty-five years, who, moreover, is an expert kayaker – and was indeed one of the earliest exponents of surf kayaking. He recommended the town he lived in, Mastic Beach, as a place to find an affordable house, observing that it had among the lowest real estate prices on the island. He was right: Mastic Beach is a rather run-down town about one and a half hour's drive from the city, mainly populated by skinny men with ponytails and tattoos and distraught women who could drop a few pounds, comparably tattooed (Drastic Mastic, is its nickname). It's blue-collar, red of neck, working-class, untouched by Manhattan money (so light-years, culturally, from the Hamptons). Cathy and I found a house there, right by the South Bay, a little run down, but cheap enough. True, Danny warned me that in his experience it was regularly flooded from the bay, which didn't sound ideal, but it was near the water and pleasant enough. I could write a novel about this tatty town now, of which I've become quite fond, but in the early days I viewed it simply as a base of kayaking operations. Mastic Beach thereafter became a major part of my life.

I remember the day I picked up my kayaks from the dank and grimy storage area at 89th Street and car-topped them out to the new house. Off to the side of the house is a room I came to call the Sport Room, in which I placed my two boats (in due course it would become much fuller), so that the boats were essentially within the home: quite proper, it seemed to me. From there I could easily carry them to the end of the street and put them in the water; it's only about thirty metres from house to bay (hence the flood danger). The bay is about half a mile across and on the other side of it is the eastern end of Fire Island, uninhabited and quite narrow, and on the far side of that is the Atlantic Ocean. So I could paddle across the bay in about fifteen minutes and walk across Fire Island to the beach. At first I would take out my yellow Dagger and paddle around in the bay, enjoying the relative peace and quiet and the natural beauty of the place: the reeds, the birds. From that point on I never set my paddle in the Hudson River again; no more inner-city kayaking for me, with the skyscrapers at my back. I started spending four months of the year in the Mastic house, during the long academic summers, after having lived exclusively in Manhattan for eight years. And this momentous change in my life had its origin in that small chunk of Styrofoam I mentioned at the beginning of the chapter: the boogie board that initially triggered my interest in water sports. It now sits in the Sport Room, largely unused but potently symbolic, nestled among the piles of other equipment that eventually accumulated. I give it a wink once in a while; it knows its place in my heart.

My next move was to figure out a way to get my surf boat over to the ocean. Various methods were essayed, but the one that worked best was as follows. I acquired an inflatable dinghy (a "Zodiac") with an outboard motor. This I kept in my driveway on a hand-pulled cart, ready to be manhandled down to the bay. I'd load it up with my surf boat and paddle and then motor over to other side of the bay, moor it, and then carry the kayak over to the beach, from which I could proceed to surf. (I'm cutting out scads of detail here about the dinghy and how to get it in and out of the water, as well as how to load it with equipment, all of which took patience and skill to master.) It moved pretty fast, so I'd be over at the beach in ten minutes. By this time I had a new surf boat, a Cobra Strike, designed by none other than my friend Danny, which was much better than anything else I'd used; I'd also learned how to surf decently. It was a nice set up, on the whole, although not without its snags and hiccups (punctured hull, lost paddle, temperamental motor). The key point is that I could now get into the water, one way or another, almost every day. I started surfing some fairly serious waves, conquering the fear, shooting along the face, knowing what can only be known by doing. Now I treated waves like friendly forces, sent to earth for my surfing enjoyment. Of course, there was still much pearling and underwater drags and getting smashed in the face by waves, but the ocean was now my playground, my sports arena. The plan had worked out, exceeding expectations. You'd think that might be the end of the upheavals, the fresh beginnings, but in fact something completely unprecedented entered my life soon after, which needs a chapter to itself. The wind.

Water is an interesting substance, two atoms of hydrogen to one of oxygen. It comes in three forms: gaseous, liquid and solid. Only within a narrow band of temperature can it exist in its liquid state. The universe, even the solar system, generally exhibits extremes of temperature that render it either gaseous or solid. On earth, most of it happens to be liquid, because of the contingent temperature of this unusual planet. It is a commonplace of chemistry and biology that without liquid water life is impossible (at least "as we know it"). Less often remarked is its contingent relation to sport. No water, no water sports: no *liquid* water, no water sports (unless we count skiing and ice skating as water sports). Surfers should reflect on how fortunate they are to live on a planet that has a climate suitable for liquid water to exist. Elsewhere H_2O is less hospitable to our sporting enthusiasms. I can just discern the outlines here of a surfer's argument for the existence of God. Or else, we are just amazingly lucky.

5. Windsurfing

All sports require three basic elements: a human body, a piece of equipment and a source of power. The part about the body is obvious, but the other two become evident on reflection. Tennis needs a racquet, high jump needs a bar, surfing needs a board, darts needs a board too, pool needs a cue, soccer needs goals, cricket needs wickets and so on. You might think running races are an exception, but even these need a finish line – as well as a suitable surface to run on. All sport is equipment-dependent, with some equipment being more complex than others. The mechanical power can have a number of sources, but something has to make something else move: it might be the arms and legs, or it might be a wave, or it might be the string of a bow, or it might be a swung bat, or it might be the wind. The body controls the power through the equipment (sport is a triadic relation, as we analytical philosophers like to say). Sailing is a sport in which power is supplied by the wind, and its equipment is a floating vessel affixed to a sail. Windsurfing is a type of sailing invented in the early 1960s that employs a very special type of equipment. In order to do it, you need intimate knowledge of the equipment and how it functions. The wind won't let you get away with anything less. Windsurfing is equipment-intensive. It's all about the gear.

I would describe windsurfing as an *advanced* sport, requiring a high level of skill that takes much time and effort to acquire (and I know). You can't just go out there and start doing it, as you can with kayaking, say. My own progress in the sport has been slow and incremental, painful even – although admittedly I only started when I was fifty. It has been frustrating, infuriating, exhausting, "character-building" (i.e. heart-breaking), exhilarating, expensive, and ultimately very satisfying. I could easily write a whole book about my windsurfing adventures, good and bad; as it is, the sport gets a whole chapter to itself. How did it begin? It began innocently enough when I was in Paragon Sports, in New York, a favourite hang-out of mine, buying some cold water gear. They had a beginner's/children's windsurfing kit for not too much money: an inflatable base or board, very thick and wide, with a miniature sail attached to a toy mast. I thought, why not give it a try? So I had it shipped out to Mastic, to be deposited in the Sport Room. I was quite content with my kayaking, but it seemed like something I might do in a casual way for a change of pace, maybe when my shoulders and back were aching from an excess of paddling.

I duly assembled the device. It was designed for maximum ease of use: the stable chunky platform to stand on and the small and easily uphauled sail. I put it in the shallow water, mounted the board, and tried to pull the sail up; the wind was light and the bay sheltered. The sail came up out of the water and spun around in the wind – as I fell backwards into the water. My kayaking in that spot hadn't prepared me for something of which I now became disagreeably aware: thick black mud on the bottom. It was like oily manure. My legs sank into it up right to the shins and it was quite hard to pull them out again – *squelch*. I climbed back on to the board and tried again, my feet black and foul-smelling. I pulled the sail all the way up this time, but as soon as I tried to sail with it I fell over again, with the same sinking and squelching. I kept trying, sometimes falling forwards over the sail, sometimes backwards with the sail on top of me. And this was to teach children on!

That was my first tormented day as a windsurfer (or sludge-sinker). On a subsequent day, the tide carried me further out than I intended and I ended up drifting away out of control, finally making landfall a few hundred yards from where I started. No paddle, you see; at the mercy of the elements and such. I had to walk home and then go and retrieve my equipment in the car. Annoying, definitely. As I was driving down a disused trail to the bay in my Land Rover, with Cathy, passing through large puddles in the road, I directed the car into what looked like yet another expansive puddle, only to find it sinking rapidly into the brackish water, which turned out to be about five feet deep. After a few seconds, dirty water started to leak through the door, and the car was totally stuck in the deep mud beneath the "puddle". Now *that* was a nasty experience (and I'd only owned the car for a couple of weeks), and all because of that wretched windsurfer! We had to have the vehicle towed away by a flat-bed truck and the insurance company declared it a total write-off, what with the salty water permeating the engine. I hereby assure you, with all due solemnity, that I never approach puddles in the road with the nonchalance of my innocent years. If I believed in such things, I'd say that someone was telling me to give up wind-surfing. But I don't, so I persisted. If at first, and so on.

Eventually I started to get the hang of it and managed to keep the mast up without falling over all the time, and even got some wind into the sail, causing forward motion. But the thing was awfully slow and cumbersome – like a mattress with a table cloth attached. So I took it to the next level: I bought a used (adult) windsurfer from a dealer, John, in Southampton. It was old-fashioned, but functional, and I wasn't yet prepared to lay out the cash for up-to-date equipment. Again, I carried it down to the bay to try it out, and again, suffered the same old rotten routine of hauling, falling, and squelching. The sail felt ten times heavier than the other one and the board was like a narrow plank in the water. After half an hour my back was hurting, my hands were chafed and blistered, and I'd taken in far too much mucky water through the nostrils. It was clearly mission impossible. Windsurfing couldn't be done; not by me anyway. But then the next day, having reflected on the subject and watched an instructional video, I gave it another try and did manage to raise the sail out of the water a couple of times without immediately toppling over. I then decided to tow the equipment out with my kayak to a place that had a sandy bottom and remained shallow as you got further out. By dint of sheer brutish determination, over a period of a couple of weeks, I contrived finally to sail the damn thing – briefly, before falling over. One salient point here is that I never took a lesson; not through foolish pride, but because there was no one in Mastic to teach me. I figured out, though, that with a lighter sail and mast the uphauling part would be much easier, so I went back to John and bought a brand new sail and rig to be attached to my old board. But it didn't take long with that combination before I realized that a new board would also make matters much easier, so I bought one of those too (total cost: over $2000!). Now that I had more modern equipment to work with, things did ease up, but I still often found myself repeatedly falling, and also being unable to sail back to the place I started from, which necessitated carrying the whole cumbersome contraption across muddy mosquito-ridden marshes back to my house (two trips – one for the sail, one for the board). There were some foul days to contend with, when everything seemed to go wrong and I'd return home exhausted, depressed, furious and filthy. Then I'd leave that windsurfing nonsense alone for a while and concentrate on my kayaking. Danny, for one, never thought I'd make it as a windsurfer (he'd tried it once years before and found it equally impossible). And yet, I'd seen people doing it: ordinary human beings too, not gods. This couldn't be a hallucination, right? Was it just me who was not cut out for it?

Now I'll truncate my windsurfing narrative and jump to the good part. I did finally learn the basics of the sport, over a period of about three years. My first sail was small (4.6 square metres), so easily handled in the wind, and the board relatively stable. I got the hang of uphauling, steering the board and keeping upright in the wind, although a strong gust would cause my skills to disintegrate alarmingly. I still had trouble aiming the board consistently upwind and so getting back to my starting-point. Also, now that I could sail, my arms would get painfully fatigued as I gripped the boom against the wind. As an extra annoyance, we had those nasty green-headed flies at certain times of the summer: the kind that like to settle on you and bite a tasty chunk out of your skin. Since the hands are fully occupied while windsurfing, it is very tricky to swat these flies off; so you either let them bite you or remove a hand from the boom for a quick swat, which usually causes you to fall off the board. No, it wasn't all fun and games out there, not by any means. For me, it was pure endurance, refusal to be defeated, patience, tiny increments of progress and the occasional breakthrough. One of the toughest challenges, after the initial stages, was learning to use the waist harness. This enables you to take the strain off your arms, because the harness, which wraps around your body, hooks on to a loop on the boom, which enables you to counterbalance the pull of the sail not with your arms alone, but with your entire body weight. You basically lean back and the sail is thereby held upright, with (ideally) your arms in a relaxed position, merely guiding the rig (i.e. sail plus mast plus boom). It took me a long time to master the harness, with the usual falling over, backwards and forwards, and the repeated uphauling. And with it came the extra calamity that you were pulled over with the sail whenever it was overpowered by the wind, since your body is attached to the rig by the harness hook. Catapulting, they call it, aptly enough. This can happen with considerable force, slamming you into the water on top of the board and rig. It's never a good moment when you feel the sail start to overpower you and you know the wind is about to body-slam you in whatever way it sees fit.

Let me then describe, with due attention to detail, how windsurfing is done, when it's done properly, so that you get a feel for what the sport is all about. You stand with legs on either side of the mast base, facing in-board, about six inches from the mast on either side, feet squarely in the middle of the board. Make sure the rig is directly downwind from you (your back is to the wind) and at right angles to the board. Don't be sloppy about this, it matters. Grip the uphaul line with both hands, knees slightly bent, back straight. Lean back and pull gently, using your legs to take most of the strain, not your lower back. Don't rush it. Make sure to keep the angle. As the rig lifts out of the water, straighten up your body, so that when it approaches perpendicular your body also does. Keeping hold of the uphaul line in one hand, the sail now flapping loosely in the wind, step back behind the mast base, while simultaneously reaching for the boom with your free hand. When you have a grip on it, let go of the uphaul line and cross your new hand over the old, pulling the boom towards you (this is called "sheeting in"). The sail will then start to catch the wind and the board will automatically move forwards. If you have a harness, now is the time to "hook in". Depending on the strength of the wind, the sail is now powered up, to one degree or another, and will cause the board to accelerate, sometimes quite rapidly. As it does so, lean back to take the strain, positioning your feet accordingly. The board will take off at a speed proportionate to the wind strength (and its own hydrodynamic character) and will start to "plane" if the wind is powerful enough, making it zip at high speed over the water. Try to keep your leading leg and back straight as you sail – no crouching forward. *Now* you are windsurfing.

The resulting experience captures perfectly what the special pleasure of sport is all about. Back in the Swinging Sixties, when I was a bearded psychology student, drinking all that coffee, lounging around, the American psychologist Abraham Maslow became something of a guru for his notion of the "peak experience". The notion was always rather vague, but the general idea is that of a "transcendent" experience, perhaps analogous to a "mystical experience". Peak experiences were supposed to correlate with maximum "self-realization". (Realizing the self then; *protecting* the self now.) At the highest levels of self-realization, you underwent a peak experience, or something along those lines (we weren't very precise in the 1960s). Presumably, a person who was highly self-realized would have peak experiences from morning until night, with no drugs ingested. He would be, in the technical term of the era, extremely *groovy*. Now, I've never had a mystical experience myself, not even a little one, but I think I know what Maslow was driving at: experiences that take you beyond ordinary daily experience, in which everything seems perfect, smooth, natural. You feel "at one with the universe". There is no alienation from the world, no cosmic awkwardness. Such experiences strike us as particularly valuable, taking us to our fullest potential as human beings. Well, I venture to suggest that windsurfing provides peak experiences in roughly this sense (it was invented in the 1960s …). I would articulate what is going on as follows. In many contexts, perhaps normally, there is a double split in our being: the mind split from the body, and the body split from the world around it (i.e. nature). We are awkwardly tethered to our bodies, and we are awkwardly situated in the world. The mesh isn't quite right: the body doesn't do as it is commanded by the mind, and nature is at odds with the body. When I was learning to windsurf (or learning other complex athletic skills) I knew what I had to do with my body, but often failed to do it; and, more poignantly, I couldn't get the world to cooperate with my body. I felt out of sync with my body and with nature. The world had it in for me, it seemed. Everything was an effort, success felt like a fluke; it was a battle, with the equipment and the wind as my enemy. There was no harmony there. Most of the experiences I had weren't peak experiences, but *pit* experiences (or *shit* experiences). I felt like a poorly designed and lowly form of life: clumsy, inept, destined for extinction. *Alienated*, in a word. But once I got the hang of it, once I could hook in and lean back and plane, a completely different phenomenology took over: a feeling of flow, control, integration. I was *at one* with the equipment and the wind. No longer was it a battle against hostile forces; nature's forces were working *with* me. The old ontological fissures were gone, with mind, body and nature now functioning as a seamless whole. Integration replaced alienation.

I want to call this kind of experience a "unity experience", because it seems to me that the essence of it is a sense of being unified with things outside of you, of everything working cohesively towards the same end. You lean back on the board, snugly hooked in, arms relaxed, and the wind simply takes you on a joyride. The equipment feels like an extension of your body, and the body itself effortlessly carries out what it needs to in order to preserve the harmony. Like the experience of surfing, it's hard to put this unity experience into words, but I suspect most people have had experiences similar enough to it to know what I'm talking about (maybe sex provides something in the same phenomenological ball park, at least once in a while). The mark of this experience is that what seemed once to be forbiddingly complex now appears the soul of simplicity. A skill that seemed fractured and labyrinthine now strikes the agent as completely natural and simple, hence the feeling of flow, unity, naturalness, ease. And the greater the underlying complexity, the higher the "peak" of the experience, the more elements have become unified. Instead of fear and anxiety, there is confidence; panic gives way to peace – and yet you're perched atop a narrow piece of fibreglass, zipping forward at an amazing lick, with the wind at your back. Invisible filaments link you to the equipment and to nature, creating a new unity. This is the "ontological argument" for windsurfing: the creation of a new entity – man-windsurfing.

Athletes often speak of being "in the zone": the place where everything goes right, nothing is a strain, invincibility rules. Implicit in this idea is a contrast: being *not* in the zone. This is the place where concentration is necessary, slips are common and you feel like a klutz. While learning a sport you're not much in the zone; you're generally way outside the zone (flailing away in the anti-zone). But acquiring the skill in question puts you in a position to have in-the-zone experiences, and these experiences strike athletes as particularly valuable. They make the struggle worthwhile. My story of windsurfing illustrates the transition from struggle and disunity to smoothness and unity. I could easily have given up at the beginning, accepting the inevitable fractures at the Heart of Being, but I persisted, so that now windsurfing *Dasein* (as Heidegger would put it) is a very important part of my life. I get to have those unity experiences remarkably often. I glimpse that peak (*sans* mysticism). Things are, in a word, *groovy*.

What I have just been saying raises an interesting question about what makes something valuable. We observe that some people seem to take a great deal of pleasure in a certain activity, such as windsurfing, and we wonder what makes them value it so. We notice that this activity is an instance of a certain general category, namely *sport*. Then we ask what makes something of that category valuable, that is, we ask after the value of sport as such. We come up with a certain answer, and then infer that what makes the specific activity we started with valuable is that it is an instance of the general category whose value we think we have identified. In other words, we move from the specific to the general, and then seek an account of value geared to the general. We say that windsurfing is valuable, say, because it is an example of sport, and sport is valuable because *blah blah*. We thus assume that the general category has value as such and that whatever value a member of that category possesses is conferred *by* being a member of the general category. In this fashion, we might suppose that (a) sport in general is valuable because it gives rise to peak experiences and (b) windsurfing is a sport – so that the value of windsurfing is that it gives rise to the peak experiences characteristic of sport. On this account, the value of the particular sport is exhausted by whatever it has in common with other sports: nothing *specific* to it accounts for its value. Here's an analogy. We notice people valuing a particular work of art, say the *Mona Lisa*. We wonder what it is about this work that people value. Observing that this entity falls into the category *art*, we enquire what makes things of that category valuable. That is, we seek the value of art in general. Suppose we come up with an answer (and philosophers of art know how hard it is to produce an answer of such generality) – as it might be, art as a category is educational/pleasurable/inspiring. Then we infer that what makes the *Mona Lisa* valuable is that, like art in general, it has the chosen characteristic; its value then derives wholly from what it shares with *other* works of art. The value of the specific thing is derived from the value of the general category it exemplifies.

It seems to me that this is a very dubious procedure, logically speaking. We want to know what the value of sport is, that is, of those activities that we group under this heading. Why not reply to this question as follows? The value of sport in general depends on the value of the particular activities that we call sport. It's not that windsurfing is valuable because it's an *instance* of sport; rather, sport is valuable because windsurfing is an example of what sport is. In other words, we should seek the value of sport in *particular sports*. This allows us to discover – what seems to me undeniably true – that the value of a particular sport depends essentially on the details of *that sport*. This is partly why I have lavished so much attention on the specifics of sports in this book, instead of proceeding at a high level of generality, as if the value of individual sports could be excogitated purely from the *general* concept of sport. As I noted in the opening chapter, *sport* is a family resemblance concept, covering a wide variety of different activities, and it is doubtful that any useful general definition can be given of the concept. If that is so, it is doubtful that we can come up with an entirely general – and illuminating – answer to the question of what makes sport as such valuable. *It depends on the sport.* Maybe we can come up with some rough generalities, but it is unlikely that we'll find something that all and only sports have in common, and that exhausts the value of any specific sport. To make the point concrete, surely the value of windsurfing has everything to do with wind, water and the specific equipment used, which are not to be found in cricket or tennis, say. Some people may find special value in the competitiveness that is part of many sports, but not all sports are inherently competitive, and those that are may be valuable for reasons more specific than competitiveness in general. It may be competition *in tennis* that specifically appeals to someone, and not competition in tiddlywinks. This incidentally explains why people tend to like some sports and not others. If the value of all sports were the same, wouldn't people be indifferent with respect to the individual sports they enjoyed? But in fact people value one sport more than another precisely because they find a specific value in the one sport that they don't find in the other. Each sport has its own specific rules, conditions, demands, equipment and so on, and these specifics are what confer value on the sport in question; *not* the fact that every individual sport is an instance of the universal Sport (as Plato would have it) and that universal has value in and of itself. Indeed, we will be in danger of finding *no* value in sport if we insist that whatever value it has must derive from the general category and not from individual instances of that category. For it is not clear that there is *anything* of value that is common to all the things we call "sport". The value is case-dependent.

I can put the point in more technical philosophical language. Each sport has its own specific phenomenology: the experiences characteristic of engaging in it. These will typically be visual and kinaesthetic, but other senses may be involved too. Specific skills are employed, and these too have their specific phenomenology. Thus, for example, there is the experience of hitting a forehand drive in tennis, which depends on the precise kinaesthetic and other sensations involved. These experiences are individuated by their objects: by the things they are experiences *of* (philosophers call this *intentionality*). The individuating objects will include the body and its

85

movements, the equipment and its deployment, the location of the activity and so on. So, in windsurfing, the experiences are individuated by wind, water, board, sail and harness, as well as the posture and muscular contractions of the body. Obviously, these experiences are specific to windsurfing, and I contend that they are what make windsurfing valuable in the particular way it is. We can't really slice off a level of experience that windsurfing shares with tennis, say, so that we can declare the value of both to depend on that experiential slice. Such a slice probably doesn't exist, and if it did it would be far too general and abstract to constitute the value of either activity. Instead, we must seek the value of each sport in the details of that sport: in the objects that individuate the experiences characteristic of the sport in question. Why do I keep learning new sports? Because each affords a different type of experience that I value for what it is. If the new sports were valuable only for what they share with the old ones, it isn't clear what the point would be in learning them. So, yes, the ideas of "peak experiences" and "unity experiences" are all well and good, but we must remember that they come in very different forms, and that the particular form they come in is integral to their value. In short, you can't gain access to the value of windsurfing unless you learn to windsurf; ten pin bowling won't do it for you.

But there are less painful and frustrating ways to do it than my way: self-taught, in muddy water, with unsuitable equipment. Take lessons from a qualified instructor, using beginner's equipment, in favourable conditions. It won't remove all the pain and frustration, but it should save the back and hands from excessive punishment. Nowadays, I sometimes teach friends the basics and know how to make it as easy as it can be (and I don't even charge them!). Even though it takes quite a while until you can ride hooked in at decent speed, it's possible to enjoy the stages leading up to that point. Learning itself is enjoyable. In the next chapter, I shall take windsurfing a stage further, even to the point of *foot straps* – an essential component of advanced windsurfing phenomenology. And there are other sports yet to be explored.

By becoming a windsurfer I have entered into a new understanding with the wind. Before, the wind was a matter of indifference to me, or a nuisance if I wanted to go kayaking. Now I notice the wind always: its strength, direction, consistency. When I'm out windsurfing I need a finely tuned sensitivity to the wind, in all its peculiarities; staying upright and on course depends on it. But even when I'm not windsurfing, I'm aware of the wind, evaluating its potentialities. Thus, this sport has alerted me to a natural phenomenon to which I wouldn't otherwise have paid much attention (much as surfing has made me aware of the dynamics of waves). It has brought me closer to nature. And not just as a passive observer, but as an agent – as a transmitter of natural forces. I *know* the wind in a way I didn't before. Such knowledge has its own intrinsic value.

6. Miami sport

I never thought I'd leave Manhattan. I had lived there for fifteen years, quite happily, five of them with my house in Long Island, hub of my sporting activities. I'd reached the point where I had seven kayaks in Mastic, three long and four short, three windsurfers, two surf boards, a table tennis table, a mountain bike, two traction kites (of which more later), two skateboards (off-road and on), roller-blades, a discus, a javelin, a pole vaulting pole, a pair of air rifles, several tennis racquets, my original boogie board and assorted accessories. Oh yes, I also owned a nineteen foot power boat, a Monterey, originally intended for water skiing, as well as my Zodiac. In the summers, from May until September, I'd be there, content-edly working at philosophy in the mornings and doing sports in the afternoons (usually with some more work before dinner). I found this routine conducive to intellectual labour and wrote several books in Mastic Beach (*The Making of a Philosopher*, *Mindsight*, *The Power of Movies*, *Shakespeare's Philosophy*). It was a pretty agree-able life: no complaints (despite the mud and the mosquitoes). But then the summer would come to an end and I'd have to go back to the city and to teaching, with only the odd weekend to prolong my summer routine. Hardly a death sentence, to be sure, but it would be eight months before I could properly resume my athletic life. Those months could feel awfully long, and fiercely cold, and I'd find myself longing for the summer to begin. I did go on ski trips in the winter, but they only lasted a few days and anyway didn't substitute for my aquatic enthusiasms. I would also take trips to the Caribbean or

Florida in search of warmth and water in the dead of the New York winter, but there was only so much time (and money!) to spend on such palliative diversions. I was leading a double life – my summer Mastic life and my winter Manhattan life – and the contrast was stark, and eventually not sustainable. During the winter months, my athletic activities were largely confined to the gym, pumping and grunting, with those ski trips and hockey games as occasional treats. And the trouble was, it simply wasn't enough. I loved New York, yes, but it just wasn't doing it for me any more. I needed year-round peak experiences. I needed an uninterrupted outdoor athletic life.

So when I had the opportunity to move to Miami I decided, after some hesitation, to seize it. I suppose the decisive moment came when I was visiting there in February 2004, escaping a particularly vicious New York winter, and I went windsurfing on Key Biscayne in eighty-five degree temperatures. The insidious thought presented itself: *I could do this all year.* That thought was very hard to dislodge. And so I moved from Rutgers University to the University of Miami in the winter of 2006. This meant moving from the Upper West Side of Manhattan, with its proximity to the Hudson River, to a place by the beach in Miami, with the Atlantic Ocean at my back door. My sympathetic reader will understand and appreciate the peculiar importance I attach to proximity to the water, so I picked a place to live that is literally a stone's throw from the ocean, in Miami Beach. Moreover, I so arranged it that I could store my equipment in a cabana facing the beach, to be carried a short distance to the water, while living on the forty-third floor of a condominium building (the Blue Diamond, to be precise – where I'm writing this book). I now look out over the azure ocean from a great height all year round, and I can kayak and windsurf to my heart's content. If it weren't for that flimsy rectangle of Styrofoam, I'd still be high and dry in Manhattan – no great tragedy, admittedly, but certainly a very different proposition. It was sport that did it, fundamentally. Sport changed my life.

But I'm going to set the water aside for a while, alluring as it is (I see it now from my window and can feel its visceral pull), and take up a theme that has recurred in this narrative: tennis. As you will recall, tennis entered my life at around age fifteen, when it evoked a brief burst of infatuation, only to hibernate over the next forty years, with occasional returns from its slumbers. In Oxford, in New York, in Nantucket, in Puerto Rico – in these far-flung locations tennis would momentarily re-enter my life, tantalizingly, seductively. But it was more frustrating than fulfilling: she came, and then she left – just as I was getting to know her. With twelve months between games, and no systematic coaching, your tennis doesn't improve much; it remains at the same dismal level of wild smashes, baffling net stops, weak backhands and putrid serves. I wasn't a *terrible* tennis player – I could hold a rally and put some topspin on my forehand (table tennis had taught me that) – but my mistakes were legion and my successful shots clumsy. What was worse, I couldn't figure out what I was doing wrong. I just seemed naturally bad at it. Nothing clicked. Something clearly had to be done. This just couldn't go on. As it happens, the Blue Diamond has its own tennis court, which is not much used; I could simply take the elevator down and be on the court in minutes. The problem was, I had no partner to play with. All I could do was practise my awkwardly cramped serve, alone (out there in the anti-zone). Two events took care of the problem. First, I contacted the local tennis pro and arranged to have some lessons with him. Secondly, one day when I was forlornly hitting serves by myself, a guy came out onto his balcony and asked if I'd like to hit with him. Sure, I said eagerly, and we started to play, quite regularly. That's how I met David and Greg, respectively; and my sporting life entered a brand new phase. Tennis came flooding back, like the lost love it had always been, with all the ardour of adolescence still clinging to it. Now the water had some competition for my athletic affections.

David is Mexican, but was born in Connecticut, now living in Miami. He's medium height, in his late thirties, with a close-shaved head and penetrating brown eyes. In addition to being a tennis pro, he's also a musician and songwriter of conspicuous talent (he gave me his self-recorded CD early on): so not your typical tennis instructor. For a while he was a professional soccer player in England. He also used to be a dive instructor in Cancun. He knows sport. I told him at our first lesson that I wanted to learn how to play well, so he shouldn't humour me and allow me to play pat-ball. I needn't have worried. The first thing he did was make me play "mini tennis", standing just behind the service area and keeping the ball inside that area – hitting it softly and accurately. I was predictably bad at this too. He observed me carefully with those alert eyes of his before offering any critique or instruction. We obviously had a lot of work to do. "Turn. Get the racquet back. Follow through. Get back in position." After about twenty minutes of this, a marathon of patience on his part, he let me back up to the baseline. From his big basket of balls, he sent one after another to my forehand (backhand wouldn't come until much later). The first thing he corrected was my starting stance. Don't stand there relaxing, with the racquet hanging loosely by your side, somewhere in the rough vicinity of the centre, but stand right in the middle of the court, just behind the baseline, both hands gripping the racquet, pointing it straight forward – *poised*. It took me a while to absorb this elementary lesson, bad habits being what they are. When he hit a long ball to me, I'd step back to take it low, letting the speed go off the ball: elementary common sense, you'd think. "Don't back up," he instructed. That meant I had to strike the ball immediately after the bounce, when it was close to the baseline, which makes the stroke much more difficult to control. Do you think David had to say this to me only once? No, he had to say it to me *dozens* of times; I just kept backing up, apparently couldn't help it. Then there was my standard method of handling a high ball. When it came to me at shoulder height, sometimes lower, my preferred strategy was to hit it with a forehand slice. This stroke had served me well against other mediocre players and was perhaps the most effective in my game. Besides, it was the only way I *could* hit a high ball. How *else* are you supposed to deal with it? You chop at it, right, get the thing under control, and hopefully engineer a nice little drop shot to wrong-foot your opponent. As soon as I executed this dinky shot, getting the ball in too, David summarily banned it: I just wasn't allowed to hit forehands that way any more. So he removed the best shot from my game, or so it seemed to me. From now on I had to hit balls like that with a topspin forehand, brushing the ball upwards with the racquet face. I found this virtually impossible and whacked the ball out nearly every time. Meanwhile, I wasn't preparing adequately before the ball reached me. I'd wait until it bounced before I brought my arm back for the strike. I needed to get into striking position much sooner. "Racquet back. Prepare." How many times did David have to shout these words to me across the net? Ten? Fifty? It must have been hundreds of times. I also had a regrettable tendency to stand with both feet perpendicular to the baseline, facing forwards, while hitting the ball. "Turn. Left foot in front." He also had to yell this at me innumerable times. My body just didn't *want* to turn. Forget turning, it said. My left hand would dangle limply in front of me as I hit the ball, as all beginners' left hands do (assuming they are right-handed). "Left hand up in front." He had to say this count-less times. When I'd run for the ball, I'd run through the stroke, instead of planting my feet firmly and hitting it from a stationary position. "Stop. Don't move the feet. Simplify." This until his voice was hoarse. My feet would either move when they shouldn't or not move when they should. Whose feet *were* they? I tried, I really did, but at the beginning of each new lesson David would have to come over to my side of the court, feigning patience, and arrange my body yet again in its proper form, which I'd somehow forgotten during the preceding seven days. Racquet back, turn, left foot forward, left hand out in front, feet planted, follow through over the left shoulder. That was just the forehand drive, you understand. There was just so much to remember! Not to mention keeping your eye on the ball and actually getting the bugger in. So my tennis education began, and it was like learning to walk all over again; or learning to *cry* all over again. I was fifty-five years old and couldn't walk – that's what it felt like. What about those good tennis years as a teenager? I was rubbish then too, of course; I just didn't realize it. I'd now say that it takes at least two years of constant practice and proper coaching to become even a decently proficient tennis player.

Concurrently with my weekly lesson from David, I started hitting with Greg, about three times a week. Greg is a big guy, a professional poker player, and no mean tennis player (powerful two-handed backhand). I was not his ideal partner, but he hung in there. We started playing in the early summer, in the south Florida heat, usually at noon (couple of mad dogs barking in the distance). After an hour or so with Greg, no part of my clothes remained dry: not just the shirt was soaked, but the shorts and socks too. Afterwards, it would be at least an hour before I stopped perspiring. Gallons of liquid were needed to re-hydrate. I found it extremely demanding and had to take frequent drink and leg breaks. Greg can hit the ball fast and consistently, so I had plenty of opportunity to work on my strokes. What David had striven to teach me on Wednesday I diligently practised with Greg for the rest of the week. He hit many high-bouncing balls, which I had great difficulty returning, but I refused to play them with my old chop shot. I also couldn't place the ball at all, being content simply to keep it within bounds. Greg and I never played real games at first, which was good for me, but once, in preparation for an upcoming poker tournament, he suggested we play a series of games in which he would give me $10 for any game I won and I would give him $1 if he won; he wanted to hone his competitive edge for the big-money event. By some miracle, I came out even after ten games (you can do the maths).

In addition to playing Big Greg, I used to go to the court on my own to practise strokes, just bouncing the ball myself and hitting it.

This way I didn't have the taxing task of having to run for the ball and hit it back to someone, which always seemed to abolish whatever technique I had so painstakingly acquired; I could concentrate purely on my form. I think this helped me a good deal and would recommend it to any novice player. It even helps to stand in your yard with just a racquet and practise strokes, with no ball to worry about. After about six months of David, Greg and solitary practice I started to have the game of tennis under some sort of rudimentary control, and David had to shout at me less and less. Finally, after some forty years of ineptitude, I could hit a forehand drive tolerably well, with pace, topspin and accuracy. It was not a killer shot, to be sure, but a respectable one; not one that made me groan with embarrassment. My technique has since improved dramatically, although it is still very much a work in progress. But there was also the question of stamina. David started to move me around the court, side to side, into the net and back to the baseline. Since he is remarkably skilled at placing the ball, this entailed an excruciating amount of multi-directional running on my part. It totally exhausted me. After a few minutes of rushing around like that, I'd be finished for the day, especially in the kind of heat we played in. But he made me keep playing ("Just two more balls!") and eventually it became less excruciating – although it's never exactly comfortable. Of course, my technique would disintegrate under this kind of pressure, with many a stab and lunge, and sometimes a reversion to that despised old chop (he'd call a halt to the rally when that happened). Gradually, I learned how to hit a running forehand drive: racquet up and back while running, bend the knees on the stroke, follow through, straight back to the centre position for the next shot.

Notice that so far there has been no discussion of backhand, or volley, or serve, or actual competitive games. David needed a full six months to work on my forehand first. I didn't think my backhand would need as much work as my forehand, but of course it did. As usual, the feet were the main fault point: I had to get the right foot forward, put my weight on it, and keep the proper distance from the ball as I struck it. None of this was child's play and I had to endure David's dead-on imitation of my natural backhand stroke: doubled-up, back turned to the net, racquet jammed up against the body, zero follow through – the usual rubbish. Just to give the ball a little topspin on the backhand is tough. The whole thing had to be reconstructed from the ground up, like a decrepit building, but by now I can give a decent impression of someone hitting backhand drives as if not in a complete panic (I've even come to prefer them to backhand slices). With respect to the serve – that shivering vortex of malefaction for most beginners – David gave me some basic pointers and my method has been to go out on my own and hit serves for an hour at a time, one ball after the other. After clocking some twenty hours of this monomania, I now have an acceptable serve, although I tend to lose it during actual competition. My net volley game is still in its primitive stages, and I much prefer to stay back and hit from the baseline. But one day I'll make a determined assault on it, mark my words. Even the best players have to steel themselves to approach the net, with its high-stakes arithmetic, its capacity for humiliation.

The serve enables me to make an important general point. Even the top players in the world can't get their first serve in all the time; often they are happy with a 60 per cent success rate. Think about it: these people have been playing tennis since they were children, they play for hours a day, their whole life is devoted to tennis, they want desperately to win, they are paid a lot of money for winning, they have the best coaching and facilities in the world – and they *still* can't get their first serve in! Wouldn't you think their success rate ought to be, what, about 98 per cent? All you have to do is serenely stand there, throw the ball up in front of you, and then hit it into a largish area only a few metres away. Of course, you need to hit the ball hard to be competitive, but shouldn't practice make perfect? Surely a machine could be designed that could throw the ball up at just the right angle, swing a racquet round to strike it just so, and propel it into the service area; it's just a problem in elementary Newtonian mechanics, after all (force, height, angle). It's not as if quantum indeterminacy lies behind all those botched serves! But the human body just finds it incredibly difficult, evidently. The serve is affected by so many variables, physiological and other, that even the experts can't master it. Serving is like predicting the weather: a case-study in chaos theory. So what hope do you and I have? Obviously, the human being was not born to serve.

Here's how you are supposed to do it. First place your weight on your leading foot, positioned at an angle to your back foot, the feet about twelve inches apart. Bounce the ball a couple of times in front of you, then ease your weight on to your back foot as you lift your left hand (if you are right-handed) to toss the ball into the air just in front of you, keeping your arm outstretched. Then swing your racquet from behind your head and strike the ball with a swift downward motion – shifting your weight back on to your front foot – thereby sending it into the desired area. It sounds easy, but just try it: you won't succeed, I guarantee. Unless you've practised serving a lot, with instruction, putting your heart into it, the chances are you'll execute some horrible little dance that will send the ball flying over the back fence or low into the net. To learn the correct action two conditions are paramount: first, you need to be able to analyse every last detail of your body's movements; secondly, you need to exercise appropriate corrective self-criticism. The first is a cognitive achievement: an affair of knowledge. The second is principally an issue of character: being willing to admit imperfection and working hard to rectify it. Chronically lousy servers refuse to accept that they don't know how to do it: somehow, they feel convinced, malevolent nature contrives to rob them of a great ringing first serve; it has nothing to do with their own ineptitude. They are just having a bad day, that's all; deep down, they have a terrific serve. So the first thing you need is humility, lashings of it. Then you need boundless patience as you strive to correct your manifold and grievous imperfections. But patience, humility and determination won't help unless you know what you're doing. You have to pay very close attention to your body, maybe invite someone else to help you analyse it, and remain self-aware as you execute the stroke. In all the sports in which I've engaged this combination of self-knowledge, humility and self-criticism are essential, but in the tennis serve they are particularly salient, because of the extreme technical difficulty of the skill. You can count yourself as having made significant progress when you miss and can say just what you did wrong. It's when you *can't* say that you're in trouble, either because of a cognitive limitation or a flaw of character. Then you don't know what you don't know. And isn't this a model of other human activities, where the consequences can be graver than merely a lost point? You always need to know exactly what you're doing and be able to correct your mistakes. Wars have gone terribly wrong for less. To be ignorant of self and incorrigible on top of it: that's *not* the way to be. Self-awareness and self-criticism: the very marks of civilization. The tennis serve is civilization in microcosm.

I have been dwelling at length on the mechanics of tennis – and you know how I love mechanics – but there is also the matter of tennis aesthetics. Here I cannot do better than quote that great tennis commentator, Vladimir Nabokov (how I would have loved to hear his commentary at Wimbledon!). It is that pivotal moment in *Lolita* where our slippery narrator, the incorrigible and self-ignorant Humbert Humbert, finally breaks through the wall of his own solipsism and sees his beloved "nymphet" as she really is for the first time – on a tennis court. "But all that was nothing," he writes, adverting to Lolita's dancing:

absolutely nothing, [compared] to the indescribable itch of rapture that her tennis game produced in me – the teasing delirious feeling of teetering on the very brink of unearthly order and splendor ... She would wait and relax for a bar or two of white-lined time before going into the act of serving, and often bounced the ball once or twice, or pawed the ground a little, always at ease, always rather vague about the score, always cheerful as she so seldom was in the dark life she led at home. Her tennis was the highest point to which I can imagine a young creature bringing the art of make-believe, although I daresay, for her it was the very geometry of basic reality ... The exquisite clarity of all her movements had its auditory counterpart in the pure ringing sound of her every stroke. The ball when it entered her aura of control became somehow whiter, its resilience somehow richer, and the instrument of precision she used upon it seemed inordinately prehensile and deliberate at the moment of clinging contact. Her form was, indeed, an absolutely perfect imitation of top-notch tennis – without any utilitarian results ... I remember at the very first game I watched being drenched with an almost painful convulsion of beauty assimilation. My Lolita had a way of raising her bent left knee at the ample and springy start of the service cycle when there would develop and hang in the sun for a second a vital web of balance between toed foot, pristine armpit, burnished arm and far back-flung racket, as she smiled up with gleaming teeth at the small globe suspended so high in the zenith of the powerful and graceful cosmos she had created for the express purpose of falling upon it with a clean resounding crack of her golden whip ... It had, that serve of hers, beauty, directness, youth, a classical purity of trajectory ...   (Nabokov 1991: 231–2)

"Oh, *my*", one feels like saying. And so Humbert's commentary ecstatically continues, dilating, digressing, noting laconically at the midway point: "I suppose I am especially susceptible to the magic of games" (*ibid*.: 233). I'll say you are, old chap. The narrator is celebrating the beauty of his adored Lolita in this passage, but he is also hymning the beauty of the game she is gracing with her participation – or choosing to highlight her beauty by placing it in this context. The echoes of the holy and supernatural are plain enough, shockingly so, and the reference to magic evokes the other-worldly aspect of the sport. Nabokov, a keen tennis player himself, obviously feels the beauty of the game, and chooses to describe Humbert's spasm of moral vision against this backdrop (he has been more or less a moral leper up to this point). I cannot myself claim wholly to reproduce Lolita's pure beauty on the tennis court, but I flatter myself that I can now, at least in a small way, participate in the aesthetic quality of the game (I have some nice tennis togs at least). And surely the pleasure of watching someone like Roger Federer on a tennis court is in large part aesthetic: he just *looks* so wonderful, as he moves, swings, and strikes – graceful, precise, elegant, poised. His forehand is surely a work of art, ranking up there with Michelangelo's *David*.

You might protest, "You're taking it all too seriously – it's just a *game*, after all! It's just playing, recreation, mucking about." The implication here is that what is merely play cannot also be serious. But it is that very combination that makes sports like tennis the unique experience they are. Certainly, tennis, like other sports, is a form of play, and play is something opposed to work – it is an alternative to work. But why should we downplay play? In play, we stand apart from our daily life of work and responsibility, entering a "magical" world with its own rules and goals. Play is universal in human culture, and obviously children delight in it (as do many animals). Don't knock play: it has its own intrinsic value. I think it's a mistake to seek to justify play as a mere prelude to work, as if it could be worthwhile only if it helps train us for the serious business of *not* playing. This is the idea that we play *so that* we can work (otherwise known as the Protestant work ethic). Art is serious and worthwhile too, without having to justify itself as an adjunct or preliminary to work. It is as philistine to downgrade play as it is to downgrade art on the grounds that neither is "serious". Isn't it better to regard work as something we do so that we can play? And why are play and seriousness seen as mutually exclusive anyway? Can't we be serious *in* play? Some people disdainfully refer to items of sports equipment as "toys", as if using them could only be childish or worse. Then we derive the sentiment that engaging in sports is just "playing with toys". (I've noticed that the very people who talk this way often have an inordinate interest in *furniture* – as if this were not also a "toy".) Play is a vital part of any full life, and a person who never plays is worse than a "dull boy": he or she lacks imagination, humour and a proper sense of value. Only the bleakest and most life-denying puritanism could warrant deleting all play from human life. Sport, it is true, is an affair of the body, and the Christian Church has historically been chary of it; in the middle ages, indeed, Plato's inclusion of athletics in a proper education was deemed improper. But presumably these days no one is such a killjoy as to prohibit sport because of its emphasis on the body, as opposed to the (supposed) immortal soul. Today, in fact, it is more likely that the puritanical mind will advocate sport as an *alternative* to sex, on the (to me, dubious) grounds that sport tires you out for sex. It's interesting that we speak of "foreplay", as if sex were itself a type of play; and then there's that use of the word "score" to denote sexual conquest. There is an affinity here, to be sure, but it would be a very stern matron indeed who disapproved of sport because of its sexual connotations. Play offers us a kind of freedom, a zone of activity in which daily burdens can be lifted. Losing a war or a job can have very real consequences for well-being, but losing at tennis is at most a blow to the ego – not the body. In sport we transcend the quotidian, if I may put it so; we rid ourselves of the shackles of ordinary existence. Sport, like art, is a type of free play of the imagination – a holiday from the Unbearable Heaviness of

Being. Let's praise it for that, not disdain it. Play is part of what makes human life worthwhile, and we should seek to get as much out of it as we can.

The ultimate defence of sport – if defence be necessary – must be that it produces happiness. It undoubtedly *does* produce happiness – as well as disappointment, frustration and occasional injury. People wouldn't do it if it didn't, not on the scale they do, and with the enthusiasm. Elementary, my dear Watson. There is no very good theory of what happiness is, unfortunately, but we know it when we see it. All the talk about peak experiences and the athlete's "high" and the satisfaction to be derived from sport attest to its ability to produce happiness. Moreover, the happiness is *internal* to it; it's not just that sport keeps you fit and healthy and *that* makes you happy. We are made happy by sporting activity itself: by tennis, by windsurfing, by basketball, by darts even. The exercise of athletic skill is a source of happiness. You are happy *that* you hit the ball so well, *that* you got a bull's-eye, *that* you caught that wave, and *that* you cleared the bar. The very content of the happiness refers to the activity in question; it isn't merely that you get a happy feeling *while* you play – you are happy *in playing*. As philosophers would say, the "intentionality" of your happiness includes the athletic activity itself, not its supposed consequences, desirable as these may also be. Sometimes nowadays people try to sell sport as if it were like a diet; not as something good in itself, but only as a means to a desirable end – say, health and longevity. I think this underplays the value of sport considerably: sport is worthwhile *intrinsically* – for its own sake. It's not a regrettable necessity, like taking an aspirin – a disagreeable means to a worthwhile end – but a welcome diversion in its own right: a pleasure not a task. Diets aren't fun: sport emphatically is.

My aquatic activities proceeded apace in Florida; not surprisingly, as this was a large part of my reason for moving there. Now I can windsurf all year round in the warm and welcoming (and un-muddy!) ocean simply by walking to the beach with my equipment. To further my windsurfing ascent, I decided to take a lesson, something I should have done long before. As I've remarked, by this time I could sail pretty well, hooked in, not falling off, at high speed. But certain more advanced techniques were still beyond me. So I met up with Jim, the dealer I'd bought my windsurfing gear from in Miami, on Virginia Key one windy Sunday morning. My mission: water starts, gibing and foot straps. These are actually bread-and-butter skills for any windsurfing enthusiast, but for one reason or another I hadn't put much effort into mastering them: too busy having a good time sailing, I suppose. Water starts are the way to get sailing without having to uphaul the sail, and are certainly a far more elegant method of getting into position on the board. Roughly speaking, you use the wind to lift you up onto the board with the rig in your hands. It's quite a complicated manoeuvre and I struggled for at least an hour with Jim trying to achieve what he performed so effortlessly, but eventually I managed it a couple of times: the sail just hoists you up out of the water and you end up standing on the board slicing gracefully forward. Gibing is a way of turning the board round by stepping round the mast, while pointing the board downwind. It's incredibly hard to do, no question. I was re-introduced to the joys of repeatedly falling off and having to uphaul the sail: the sore back, the reddened hands, the swearing. But it was the foot straps that were the true revelation that fine Sunday morning. I'd viewed them as distinctly optional, useful for carrying the board, but not essential for happy sailing. I'd tried inserting my feet into them a couple of times in Mastic, but it was hard to do and the board would immediately turn into the wind and lose power. Jim insisted I learn foot straps, however, making me sail at speed downwind and then thrust my feet into the straps in just the right way, which again is no simple matter. The upshot was that when I went back to my own equipment on the beach a few days later, I made myself use the foot straps: and the difference was phenomenal, especially in strong wind. Now that I was rooted fast to the board I gained speed far more quickly, being able to use my feet more effectively. Planing at speed in the foot straps was a dream. The sense of being at one with the equipment was far more intense. My exhilaration level was through the roof. I felt my windsurfing had reached a new peak that day, seven years after starting the sport. I still have to work more on gibing and water starts, but I've had the best windsurfing sessions of my life since mastering foot straps. Thanks, Jim. I've learned something new and valuable, expanded my practical knowledge, further fused my mind and body, and enjoyed all those peak experiences – just by sliding my feet into those straps.

I've saved until last my experiences with kiteboarding, and I have to wonder about your willingness to be introduced to yet another sport – with its own jargon and culture, its own mechanics and aesthetics – so late in the day. But trust me, it'll be worth it, and I don't intend to hit you with too much on the first outing. You may think you've heard about some significant athletic ordeals so far in this book, some ups and downs; now the ordeal level is about to be ratcheted up a notch. Here the mishaps take on a new and darker complexion. This will be very much a case of "Don't try this at home".

It didn't start in Miami but in Barbados. I'd travelled there one winter, when I was still living in New York, mainly in order to windsurf; but they also offered kiteboarding lessons near where I was staying, and the sport had caught my eye before. Tony was to be my instructor, a young native of the islands, handsome, self-contained and a charismatic kiteboarder and water man. I showed up at the beach early one morning, raring to go, but with a touch of the butterflies. At first I was allowed to fly only the small "training kite" to get a feel for the "wind window" and how to power and de-power the kite. After a couple of hours of that, standing on the beach in the blasting sun, Tony let me graduate to the big traction kite. I don't want to blind you with science about kiting, but there is a mass of theoretical stuff to learn before you even get your feet wet: the neutral zone, the power zone, the control bar, the power lines and flying lines, the leading edge, the chicken loop, the release mechanism, the aspect ratio. The first thing I noticed when Tony attached the big kite to my harness was how incredibly powerful it was. These kites are typically about twelve square metres in surface area and designed to catch the wind with maximum efficiency. If the kite shifted even slightly from 12 o'clock (its most neutral position), it would power up alarmingly and start to pull me inexorably forwards. People have been seriously injured and even killed by being dragged by their kite into solid objects. I can still hear Tony urgently shouting to me as the kite unintentionally picked up traction: "De-power the kite!" Frankly, the thing was totally terrifying. Cautiously, I followed my teacher's instructions (my life being in his hands) and began to be able to move the kite around the wind window under reasonable control. But the whole time I could practically taste the adrenaline in my mouth. After four hours of practice on the beach, we finally got into the water for some "body dragging": using the kite to pull you through the water on your belly, that is, without using the board. Tony swam out with me at first, gripping the back of my harness, so that he could instruct me and save me from potential problems. I managed to gain some forward momentum without crashing the kite into the water – at least for a while. The power was still formidable, but it was reassuring to be surrounded by liquidity not solidity. Still, those big surges reminded me of what I was attached to.

The critical moment came after six hours of intense instruction, when I was ready to make my first attempt at standing up on the board under power from the kite. I was on my back, alone in the water, the kite hovering above me at 12 o'clock, attached to my harness, the control bar in my hands, the board attached by its leash to my ankle. All I had to do was insert my feet into the straps, dive the kite and stand up. It had all been leading up to this stupendous climax. However, the kite started to lose position as I fiddled with the board, dipped into the power zone, violently spun me round, and then crashed hard into the ocean, yanking me with considerable force in its direction, completely out of control. I think I screamed. Tony had to swim out and rescue me and the kite. I was shaken up and badly disappointed, but not physically injured. The next day I had to leave Barbados to go back to New York, so no more kiting for now. I had learned the basics of kiteboarding, but I hadn't achieved the thing that is the point of the entire exercise: standing up on the board and riding. I had been on the very brink of that achievement, but cruel fate had deprived me of it. I trust that you, my empathic reader, can feel my pain.

So it remained for three long years, rankling from inside me. I'd missed my big opportunity, let myself (and Tony) down, utterly blown it. When I got back to New York I bought my own kite and board, naturally, intent on pursuing my new interest on Long Island in the summer. Despite some valiant attempts, however, I didn't get very far: some kite flying on the beach and body dragging in the bay, but no actual riding on the board. It wasn't until very recently, in Miami, that I finally took it a stage further. I bought myself a better kite (a Cabrinah Switchblade II), one of the new "bow kites", with a special harness, and arranged a lesson at a place called Matheson Hammock, near the university I work at. My teacher was to be Miguel, who turned out to be descended from Welsh migrants to Patagonia, a young man of calm resolve and quiet trustworthiness (important in a kiteboarding instructor). Miguel knows his kites intimately and runs his own kiteboarding company: an expert, no question. The first lesson was a refresher, to see how my kite-flying skills stood and to practise some body dragging. It went fine, although I had that old adrenaline taste in my mouth: a brew of fear and excitement. It wasn't until the next lesson that Miguel deemed me ready to try to get up on the board. First I had to learn how to keep the kite still, as I lay on my back in the water preparing to dive it: the skill I lacked back in Barbados. Miguel put the board on my feet for me, which made the process a good bit easier. After a couple of faltering attempts, I did succeed in getting myself upright on the board, but soon toppled over. I made some adjustments in the way I was flying the kite and did a little better the next time. After several attempts I was reliably managing to move forwards, standing upright, although feeling very unsteady and nervous. Genuine progress was being made. Hey, I can do this!

That's when something really bad happened. I was concentrating on the kite in the sky and the board under my feet and I didn't see another kiteboarder in the water in front of me. I ran directly into him. This is an extremely dangerous thing to do and can cause serious injury if the kites get tangled and fly out of control. Fortunately, the other man stayed calm and untangled our lines, as I showered him with apologies. I thought the worst was over when my kite suddenly started to go into a wild loop, crashing down into the water. Since I was attached to it, I was pulled hard through the water as it dipped, crashed and then climbed again, repeating the cycle, gathering power and acceleration with every revolution. I was being dragged behind it with great force, sometimes under the water, on my back, on my front, swallowing water, unable to get the kite under control. I tried to negate the kite's pull by using the de-power mechanism, but for some reason it didn't work. I was being dragged closer and closer to land – and many hard pointy objects. I *had* to disengage myself from the kite, so I resorted to disconnecting the leash from my harness, thus completely detaching myself from the whole whirling demon. Finally, the kite left me behind and blew across the bay, coming to rest in someone's dock on the far side. I swam back to Miguel, at least two hundred yards, exhausted, knocked about, feeling seriously shaken. Miguel told me that after the collision with the kiteboarder in the water a line had wound round one end of my bar, destabilizing the kite, and the only thing I could do at that point was let the whole thing go. As for the kite itself, I'd have to drive over there to extricate it, and it would probably be badly damaged. I did, and it was. This was not a good experience all round, not good at all. I'd got up on the board all right, but then that success had been quickly followed by what amounted to a near-death experience. Back on land, other kiters spoke in hushed tones of people they'd seen dragged across the parking lot, and how lucky I really was. The place Miguel had taken me to for the lesson was far from land, precisely in order to protect beginners from this type of situation. I drove home feeling discouraged and traumatized. Mud is one thing: dead quite another.

Miguel repaired my kite in time for my third lesson, which I approached not without some apprehension. This time I got up on the board moving in both directions, left and right, and managed to put the board on my feet myself, although my riding technique can only be described as *vile*. I did, however, make another mistake late in the lesson and let the kite get out of control for a while, although nowhere near as nastily as the first time – but enough to terminate the session. I left feeling marginally less terrible than the first time. Kiteboarding was proving difficult, no question. What could possess me, you might wonder, to engage in such a dangerous sport at the ripe old age of fifty-seven? It's a good question, and thank you for your concern. But I do have an answer for you: kiteboarding is the closest thing yet invented to flying like a bird. If you've ever watched someone competent doing it, you will know exactly what I mean: the kite is like a huge wing that can skim you across the water and launch you into aerial moves of stunning grace and amplitude. You should have seen Tony launch himself into the air directly from the beach, tear across the water and propel himself high above the ocean, spinning, wheeling and landing again like some sort of pumped-up eagle. How anyone can witness this spectacle and not think, *I want to do that*, is beyond me. There is something deeply thrilling about the power of these kites, and about what they can be made to do with the human organism. The sport has only been in existence for about ten years, but already it has spread across the globe; and kiters are fanatical about their sport, distant-eyed with elation and insider knowledge. It's poised for world domination, no doubt. *Richard Branson* is a kiteboarder, for heaven's sake; that has to tell you something. It has some claim to be the coolest sport on the planet. Sure, there are risks, quite big ones, but then what would you expect of flying? I expect to do much more of it, once I recover from the trauma induced by my last two attempts, that is.

I am a teacher – of philosophy. In this chapter I've mentioned, glowingly, three recent teachers of mine: David, Jim and Miguel. The role of teachers in sport is important. The teacher must impart skills, encourage confidence, protect the athlete against injury, offer constructive criticism and set an example. These are not insignificant virtues, and a good teacher of sport cannot be a mediocre human being. The relationship of teacher and pupil is unusually intimate and relies essentially on trust. I don't care for the popular image of the win-at-all-costs coach prowling the locker room, hectoring, bellowing. A good coach must be calm, quiet, clear, concerned. As a teacher of philosophy, I don't need to be worried about the physical well-being of my students, but a sports coach often has to have this uppermost in her mind. The student, for his part, must be open to instruction, humble, attentive, retentive, determined and focused on the task at hand. So there must be moral virtue on both sides of the athletic teaching relationship. It is sometimes supposed that moral character grows through the competitive element of sport. I'm doubtful about this, because of the dangers of alienation inherent in competing with other people, not to speak of the abuses to which competition so easily leads. Morality must regulate competition, rather than growing *from* competition. But I do think that the teacher–pupil relationship in sport is an unusually potent one ethically, bringing out the best (and sometimes the worst) in both parties. So, in addition to the aesthetic and mechanical aspects of sport, there is the ethical aspect, most apparent in the relationship of teacher and pupil. The happiness of the teacher as she sees the progress of the student is the clearest manifestation of this ethical element. I actually derive at least as much pleasure from teaching people to windsurf or play table tennis as I do from teaching them philosophy. The results are more palpable, for one thing.

7. Athletic investigations

In previous chapters, I have approached sport by considering in some detail a variety of particular sports, using my own experience as a jumping-off point. I have done so in the conviction that the best way to understand sport is to immerse ourselves in the specifics of individual sports, letting more general points emerge naturally, rather than trying to work out from the abstract concept *sport* what sport is all about and why it matters. For one thing, the concept is vague and not susceptible to straightforward definition (it's a family resemblance concept). For another, what is interesting and distinctive about sport resides in the nature of the particular activities that are so classified. Indeed, I needn't have employed the general category Sport at all in this book; I could have simply discussed a series of activities – gymnastics, pole vaulting, tennis, windsurfing and so on. For a third thing, sport lends itself to narrative exposition, because there is an inherent drama to it; this is why sport enjoys the media saturation it does – it's a story of stories. Every game or match is a story in itself – it has a beginning, a middle, and an end – and the process of learning a sport has its own narrative arc (will there be success or failure?). Sport, play, stories: they all go together. Also, the sports a person engages in are part of the overall story of his or her life: how it starts, where it leads. This is certainly true of my life. Trying to discuss the meaning of sport by abstracting away from the details of specific sports strikes me as a fruitless procedure.

But in this final chapter, I want to stand back from the peculiarities for a while and offer some general reflections on sport as such.

My aim is not to provide necessary and sufficient conditions for something to be a sport – that is, to talk about the *essence* of sport in general – but rather to articulate what is *typical* of sport or at least many sports. I'm not aiming to analyse the concept, picking apart its supposed constituents, but rather to explore its connection with other concepts: its friends and relatives in the great scheme of things. Wittgenstein would describe sport as one of our "forms of life", along with language, science, art, war, music and sex; I want to delineate this form, provide a picture of it. I approach it as a natural phenomenon that occupies a particular role in human life. What does it *mean* to us? How is it embedded in the human *Umwelt*?

Let's begin at the beginning, with sport and physics. I haven't explicitly brought this subject up before, but it has been implicit at several points. Sport is very Newtonian, isn't it? It's all about masses accelerating under the action of forces: $F = ma$ and all that. Sport is tangling with Newton's three laws of motion: (i) things continue in a uniform state of motion unless actively retarded or accelerated; (ii) force equals mass times acceleration; (iii) for every action there is an equal contrary reaction. In sport the human body may be the moving mass, the thing accelerated by forces (e.g. by the kinetic energy in the bent pole while vaulting); or it may be a projectile to which the player applies force (a ball, a javelin, a discus, etc.); or it may be both (like running and kicking a football). I can't think of any sports where chemistry plays a significant role, except maybe those frightful food eating contests. It's the human organism locked into a tango with Newtonian laws that constitutes athletic activity: biomechanics, in effect. These laws set the natural parameters of the game; the players operate with man-made rules in concert with nature-given laws. You have, for example, to accelerate the ball just so much that it bounces within a certain humanly constructed line. So sport mixes the cultural and the physical in a particularly intimate way: it's the juxtaposition of the normative and the natural (rules and laws). This means that an athlete must have an especially sensitive relationship to basic physical laws; she must know them intimately – not just theoretically, but practically. To be a successful athlete, you have to be an intuitive physicist, a natural Newton. You have to acquire a profound understanding of the physical forces that surround and control you: how much force of a certain kind is required to obtain just this degree of motion. This sensitivity puts you in touch with some of the most fundamental facets of the universe. Motion, mass, force: you have to become a master of those categories. That is to say, you have to learn about the universe in its most pervasive aspects. You have to have a little Newtonian homunculus nestled somewhere in your nervous system, with unimpeded access to your muscles. And when you do acquire such knowledge, essentially intuitive and practical as it is, you enter into a relationship with nature that is deep and elemental. You "Use the Force", quite literally. You are in tune with the basic laws of the universe, becoming one with it.

It is hard to avoid the conclusion that we like to do this for a reason: namely, to assert our being over the great laws of nature. We are born into a world of fixed natural laws, to which we are totally and pitilessly subject, and in the formation of which we have no say. They are the *given*. If you push us, we move sideways; if you drop us, we accelerate downwards; if we collide with a solid object, it strikes back. Above all, we are the puppets and playthings of the force of gravity. We contend with gravity at every moment of our waking life (and then we dream all night about it). This is a burden, a challenge, a peril. But in sports we play *with* these forces; we exploit them for our own human ends – fun, amusement, gain. We set up a game in which the great forces will be continually brought to bear, if not to heel – just because we feel like it. We thereby fold the impersonal into the personal. We can never change the laws, but we can at least make them serve our human ends. In tennis, say, you can call on Newton's laws in order to propel the ball into the service area, thus challenging your opponent to perform his own dance with Newton.

If you could change the laws at will, you could make sure your first serve went in every time, and at a thousand miles an hour too. But that would destroy the whole point of the game. The laws must *constrain* play. A universe without laws, or in which the human will was law, would be a universe in which sports could scarcely exist. (It's hard to imagine God playing a sport, since he is subject to no laws. Celestial ping-pong is a dubious proposition.) So we *use* the world as we find it (and also fear it) to constitute activities that serve our human purposes: amusement, competition, fitness, and so on. In this way, we get one over on nature, as it were. Sport co-opts nature, and thus asserts the human over the inhuman. Maybe we even nurture the conviction that we really have transcended nature, as with the extraordinary feat of pole vaulting.

At the same elemental level, sport requires bodily coordination. If you're not physically together yourself, you won't be able to meld with the forces of nature. Some people, as we know, are not terribly well coordinated (we call them "intellectuals"). To be well coordinated requires two things: that your body does what it is told, and that it acts as a unity. The mind must hold dominion over the body, and the body must function in a unified manner. It's hard to avoid political metaphors here. The body must not be in rebellion against its nominal ruler, the mind; and the body must not consist of warring factions, unable to operate as a whole. In other words, there must be two sorts of harmony: of body with mind, and of different parts of the body with each other. I take it harmony is a good thing; we need more of it in our lives. To be coordinated is to be harmonized: not to be at odds with your own being, fractured and disparate, all over the joint. In successfully learning a sport we achieve such coordination, which is to say internal harmony. We bring order to the state – our state. We take the body from a condition of disorganized anarchy to one of integrated focus. Surely that is a big part of the attraction of sport. You start off all over the place, your body stubbornly refusing to do as it is told, pulling you in opposite directions, and you end up sleekly unified, every-thing working to a common purpose. Unity emerges from disunity. The fragments that compose an embodied agent come together, as if several agents meld into one. We all strive not to be clumsy: we recognize that this is a not a desirable way to be. Well, sport takes this striving to the extreme, contriving new ways to replace clumsiness by coordination. And what is clumsiness but discord in the "body politic"? If clumsiness is our natural condition, our default state, then athletes strive to achieve an ideal state of anti-clumsiness. The clumsy is replaced by the coordinated. What is achieved is a kind of self-government.

Learning to be coordinated is a type of education, basic but important. As I pointed out in Chapter 1, physical education is properly so described: it is the acquisition of knowledge – specifi-cally, knowledge-how. It is a type of cognitive enrichment. But it's not just enrichment of the mind, but of the body too. Better, it's an enrichment of the *person*: that irreducible entity that combines mind and body. By training the person in physical skills, the body itself becomes infused with knowledge. And who wants an igno-rant body? We like our minds to be knowledgeable, well-stocked with information; we should also want our bodies to be similarly endowed with learning. The erudite body is a good body to have. In an overall good life, *both* mind and body should be richly informed, properly educated. (In my life as a philosopher I've known quite a few people with highly informed minds, but bodies like the proverbial blank slate.) Athletic skill is one type of bodily knowledge (playing a musical instrument is another). Or to put it more precisely: athletic skill involves the person in knowledge that is indissolubly psycho-physical. Knowing how to play tennis, say, is a skill that seamlessly combines mental with bodily accomplishments; you can't have one without the other. Our educational system should acknowledge the value of both types of education, as it has traditionally done, however imperfectly, following the model of the ancient Greeks.

I actually would quite like to teach not just philosophy but also sport, to the same group of students (and intend to do so in the next couple of years). Today we are dealing with the theoretical mind–body problem in the classroom, tomorrow the practical mind–body problem out on the playing field (or in the water). In any case, we should not disdain physical education as not being *real* education. Intelligence comes in many forms, and there is such a thing as intelligence of the body (itself of many forms).

All learning can be viewed as an expansion of the self, an incorporation of what is outside into what is inside. When you learn history or physics or biology you extend yourself beyond the boundaries that defined you before. But equally, when you learn an athletic skill you likewise expand the self: you become larger, more capacious, a fuller being. The blank slate becomes a richly illustrated text, animated too. The void becomes a plenum. You know stuff you didn't know before. You thereby become less narrow and confined, more a citizen of the universe. And the self you become is a self to be proud of: expansive, inclusive, amply endowed. The self must always be a work in progress, and lifelong learning is the way to keep it from stagnating or shrinking. Of course, as a university professor, and dedicated book-writer (the fingers tapping away), I value purely intellectual learning highly, but I also advocate the growth of the self through physical education. So here is my little morsel of self-help advice: expand the self by athletic learning (as well as the other kind). Learn quantum mechanics, by all means, but don't neglect athletic mechanics. Be all you can be – that type of thing.

In my view, the best approach to learning a sport (and engaging in a sport is always continuing to learn it) involves recognizing both its mechanical and aesthetic aspects. These are equally important, indeed complementary. You can't just go out on the tennis court and expect to hit a beautiful stroke; you have to learn the mechanics first – the exact way in which to move your body and the racquet.

You have to pay your dues mechanically. But the aesthetic aspects of the sport should always be before your mind: you should always be striving for beauty – a good stance, a smooth movement, the proper attire and equipment. In some sports the aesthetic element is dominant – figure skating, diving, gymnastics – but in all sports there is the matter of economy, elegance, style. Even boxers work on the aesthetics of their violent sport (Muhammad Ali took himself to be the greatest *and* the prettiest). Some javelin throwers are lovelier than others, believe it or not. Coordination itself inextricably combines the mechanical and the aesthetic: you have to get the details of the movement right mechanically, but the upshot is an aesthetic whole. Dancing is not dissimilar (think of Fred Astaire: the most graceful tap athlete ever), although here the aesthetic component is paramount. I never feel I have the mechanics down until the aesthetic has been exemplified. When it looks good it has been done right – roughly. The backhand in tennis is a perfect example. What do coaches shout when an action has been performed correctly? "Beautiful!"

When it looks good it also *feels* right: the first-person phenomenology has a comely shape. What is this feeling-right business? Primarily, as I've indicated earlier, it's a matter of experiencing yourself as a unity: not as an uneasy compound of mind and body, will and movement, but as a single unified entity, working as an organic whole. Indeed, I have suggested that the sense of unity extends beyond the body into the environment; it is ecological in structure. In windsurfing, say, body and mind are functioning harmoniously, but you also feel at one with the equipment and the forces acting on it. You *are* the equipment. More, you feel continuous with the wind and the water. When you're "in the zone" you're there body and soul; the distinction between the two hardly exists. You don't feel yourself to be a divided being, a Cartesian contraption made up of an errant body tenuously linked to an incorporeal mind. Body flows into mind, and mind flows into body – like a single stream. You become embodied agency – a *sui generis* ontological category. This is a somewhat godlike condition, because gods are not divided in their being (Descartes wasn't a dualist about *God*). To be a god is to be a fully unified being whose actions and intentions perfectly coincide, whose body is never in rebellion against her mind. The gods don't suffer from problems of coordination, struggling to overcome their natural clumsiness. When the gods play a game of badminton (which, I'm reliably informed, is their favourite sport – who knew!), it's all unity and flow. It is not the recalcitrant body thwarting the mind's orders. There is no such split. When people idolize their athletic heroes as gods, is it this impression of ontological unity that prompts their adulation? The outstanding athlete seems to operate on another plane of coordinated movement, above mere mortals. His body appears as the pure will in motion. This must be why it seems like an abrupt ontological descent when Roger Federer, for no apparent reason, whacks the ball awkwardly into the net. Oh, he's human after all, we think, shaken from our fantasy. His action has failed to integrate with his intention (feet in the wrong place, usually). One of the nice things about being a god is that this kind of mistake never occurs (unless, I suppose, one of the other more mischievous gods sticks a spoke in the wheel). The tennis gods never flub their second serve.

At this point my constitutionally querulous reader may well be itching to intervene. "You have been extolling the virtues of sport at some length," she might say, with a slight flare of the nostrils, "but what about all the negative things in sport? What about the commercialization, the tribalism, the injuries, the violence, the drugs, the philistinism, the terrible sports commentators?" This protest deserves a proper reply; indeed, I have a lot of sympathy with it. The spectacle of professional sport, as we have it today, is often unlovely, uninspiring and unhealthy. Pumped-up, egotistical, overpaid, irresponsible, crude: these are some of the epithets that spring to mind when considering many athletes today (and I'm only considering ten pin bowlers here). Then there are the concussions and the crippling, the fouling and cheating, the loud voices and even louder ties. What about the pharmaceutical delinquency of many top athletes? Doesn't sport today, particularly big-time athletics, wrongly elevate winning above all other values ("winning isn't everything; it's the only thing")? Winning is, in any case, at best, forcing the opponent to lose, and isn't that alienating and unkind, selfish and un-altruistic? Wouldn't society be better off if we banned sports altogether? Then children would learn to be peaceful and cooperative, read more and speak quietly and intelligently. And surely we *all* want to rid the world of those annoying commentators; that, at least, must be a non-partisan issue!

My reply to these natural misgivings is simple: what we are describing here is the *corruption* of sport, not its *essence*. Yes, the sporting impulse – the sporting *spirit*, we might say – has been corrupted and debased; but this is not intrinsic to the very nature of sport. It's an imposition from outside, from extraneous sources. The problem, simply put, is money: capitalism, commercialization. Do you think sex should be banned? Do you think sex is an inherently bad thing? I certainly hope not. That would be sad. But sex also has been corrupted, by money, by capitalism, by commercialization. Indeed, you might say that sex has always been corrupted, one way or another, without itself *being* corrupt. People see ways to make money out of sex – by pornography, prostitution, and sexual slavery – and so they corrupt it, with all manner of dire consequences. But it isn't that sex is in itself a bad thing; corruption isn't part of its very nature. Almost any worthwhile thing can be corrupted when money becomes involved (think of the big-time art market or day-to-day politics). Sport has accordingly become corrupted in our money-driven society, deformed and defiled. (For all I know, it was already a little corrupt in Plato's day, but surely the process is wider and deeper now than ever.) The desire to win at all costs is manifestly driven by the financial penalties of losing. If the team keeps losing, the fans will lose interest, will not buy tickets, and then the players won't get paid, and the boss will go bankrupt. Attracting the best athletes to a team requires paying them more than other teams will pay: but then they will end up being paid ludicrous amounts, and festooning themselves with "bling" and those maroon suits with shiny buttons. Money has that way of vulgarizing and reducing. Sport is not immune to its oily and sour charm. People will always cut corners when the financial stakes are high enough. Human nature, innit.

But none of this means that *your* engagement with sport has to be corrupt, any more than your behaviour in the bedroom has to be corrupt. You can distance yourself from the corruption and still be athletic, or sexual. (But be careful: don't let the insidious corruption all around you seep into your own psyche – which it can so easily do.) Indeed, we might reasonably feel that the essence of sport is *antithetical* to the forms it has assumed in some quarters: that this essence, in its original and pristine form, goes against the forces of capitalism and greed. (The same might be said of sex.) Sport is essentially innocent, in its primary nature, and so stands against the crass forces of the capitalist market; it is an *alternative* to rapacious capital accumulation. Play, in general, can claim to be antithetical to the single-minded pursuit of money. That's why we speak of sport as *corrupted*: because it has an intrinsic nature that is opposed to what it can become. Sport operates by values that are inherently opposed to ungoverned greed, but those values can be usurped and deformed. When sport and sex turn into work, undertaken for money, sometimes big and sleazy money, everything changes. Their essential innocence is lost. In themselves, however, these activities are logically independent of work and money. Both belong more to the category of *play*: of pleasure, recreation. As pure play, sport exists apart from its corrupt manifestations. So let's not blame sport itself for what some people have foisted on it. Our obligation is to pursue sport in its pure form, eschewing its corrupt offshoots, not ban it because it has been defiled. In any case, the excesses of professional sports – gambling, drug-taking, cheating, violence and so on – have no bearing on the individual's pursuit of athletic happiness. When I am out happily windsurfing, for example, all that is far, far away, and nothing to the point.

But two further negative aspects remain to be discussed: injury and competition. Under the first heading I'd include muscle soreness and backaches, and even psychological frustration and despair, as well as the usual torn muscles and broken bones. There seems to be a good deal that's undesirable about the athletic experience, even on my own showing (that kiteboarding accident wasn't a felicitous one). I don't think this point can be dodged or denied. No matter how careful you are, accidents will happen, sometimes serious accidents, and I understand how some people might be deterred even by the psychological suffering. "No pain, no gain", as the saying goes; or lots of pain, not much gain. I myself recently pulled a hamstring while practising water starts, which has messed up my tennis. Why not avoid the pain by foregoing the gain? Isn't it safer to stay home? The only answer can be that the gain is worth the pain. After all, even moderate exercise, such as jogging and crunches, is intrinsically rather disagreeable, producing sore muscles the next day. But the benefits outweigh the discomfort. You *might* injure yourself jogging (pot holes can be lethal), but that's a risk you're prepared to take if the benefits for health are great enough. Of course, it's folly to take on sports that are very likely to lead to serious injury (jumping off garages, say), but in a lifetime of sport I've never had anything all that bad happen to me, although I've been knocked around a little. You take the rough with the smooth, right? You might suffer while undertaking almost any worthwhile pursuit – love, philosophy or arctic exploration – but life would be duller without such activities. You must assess and manage the risks, obviously, doing your cost-benefit calculations, but I don't think you'll find that sports are vastly more dangerous than other things you willingly undertake (such as driving a car). In fact, participating in sports helps you to develop a healthy attitude towards risk, since the consequences of error or accident are usually immediate. Rashness and operating above your capacities will quickly be corrected, and it's useful to rid yourself of such tendencies. Sport is a workshop of risk management.

This brings out an important point: in sport we learn how to assess, and work within, our capacities. We learn what we can do and what we can't do. We come to know our scope and limits. This is a very valuable type of knowledge, a type that Socrates was notably anxious to instil. You have to know what you don't know, he tirelessly warned, and what you can't do, I might add. As well, you should cultivate a judicious sense of your positive abilities; don't de-value them (here is where "proper pride" comes in). This is a kind of *self*-knowledge, and of an especially valuable type. Take tennis. When people start playing tennis they always hit the ball too hard, lofting it time after time (men are particularly bad about this). It takes a while to moderate your shot so that the ball stays within bounds. Improving your shot is mainly a matter of knowing where your skill level will justify a particular degree of power; in other words, you shouldn't hit it harder than your skill level permits (spin is what enables you to combine power and accuracy). This clearly requires self-knowledge in regard to your tennis abilities. Much the same is true of intellectual abilities or even social abilities. We all know people who consistently (and risibly) overestimate their knowledge, charm, fashion sense, wit and whatnot; they lack a clear sense of their scope and limits. In sports such self-ignorance is quickly exposed; not that it always leads to a course correction – some people never learn, regrettably. The nice thing is that in sport you can work to push your limits further and further, especially once you become aware that you have limits. You identify the limits, and then you labour to expand the area within them. You work *with* your limits, acknowledging their reality, using them to increase your scope. In other words, go for it – but don't overreach.

The question of competition also calls for judicious balancing, as I've several times observed. There's no getting away from it: competition involves the elevation of one person at the expense of another. Competition is not cooperation, although it relies on a background of cooperation to make the game possible at all. You are trying to make the other person lose; and he's not going to like that, not one bit. Thus, there's an inescapable element of alienation in every competition: of you *versus* him (or her). That cannot be denied or gainsaid; it can only be mitigated. In a competition, then, your duty is to treat your opponent with special, even exaggerated, respect. You are trying to beat him, sure, but you must apply the rules fairly, scrupulously and courteously. There must be no gloating. His excellent play must be acknowledged as such. The handshake at the end symbolizes this indispensable counter-alienating attitude: we are friends, colleagues, even though one of us has won and the other lost. Winning must be embraced graciously, and losing must be accepted with good humour. I myself don't particularly go in for sports that involve competition; that's not my reason for athletic activity. For me, the exercise of skill is paramount – whether it is against someone else is incidental. But when I do compete with someone, I'm mindful of the ethical predicament, and always feel a twinge of unease when I win, although also the thrill of victory, to be sure. The competitive attitude is essentially ambivalent, or it should be. But even if you can't stand competition, that doesn't mean sport is not for you; there are plenty of non-competitive sports. There are, of course, those who believe – we mentioned them earlier – that sport is admirable precisely because it encourages ruthless competition, this being deemed a trait of modern life. Such individuals are called "ethical egoists" by philosophers, holding as they do that your only duty is to yourself: others are merely means, or obstacles, to your own advancement. Competition, for such egoists, is primarily a matter of exerting power over others, and coming out on top. Altruism is viewed as foolish or psychologically impossible. But this is a highly questionable moral philosophy, for reasons I won't here go into, and anyway athletic competition need not be conceived in such egoistic terms. If we regard competition, instead, as the best means of producing athletic excellence, then it has a higher goal than merely the assertion of one ego over another. The proper aim of competition is to win *by means of excellence*, not to win in whatever way you can, fair or foul. As I observed in an earlier chapter, to win by cheating is a violation of the very nature of athletic competition. It is basically self-refuting.

There is a great deal of failure in sporting activity. I don't just mean losing to someone else; I mean failing to execute a particular skill properly. There is a tremendous amount of miss-hitting, falling over, belly-flopping, losing possession of the ball, getting dragged through the water, crashing into the bar and so on and forth. In the course of this book, I have described numerous instances of me failing to do what I set out to do: repeatedly, embarrassingly, painfully. And I'm a naturally gifted athlete; in fact, I'm about the best all-round athlete I've ever come across, inside or outside the academy. Not that I could ever compete with a seriously competent athlete in any of the sports in which I've dabbled (and I am an inveterate dabbler). But what do you think Roger Federer is like on a windsurfer? Has he ever pole-vaulted? How good do you reckon he is at faggies? What about Tiger Woods? A nice golfer, admittedly, but can he surf-kayak, play tennis, fly a traction kite and dig worms? And so on. My point is that even I, who can pick up almost any sport with a little effort, fail all the time, especially in the early stages. (I can hear some reviewers complaining at this point about my boastfulness. To them I say: come and spend a couple of days with me, and we'll see. Other reviewers will hotly censure my parenthetically attempting to pre-empt the first sort of reviewer. To them I say: have a nice day.) Failure comes with the territory in sport. Roger himself once used to bungle his serves dreadfully and hit wild volleys (when he was about five). There is no success in sport without failure. Failure is the mechanism of success.

Compare Karl Popper's theory of the growth of scientific knowledge, or Charles Darwin's theory of evolution. Both theorists assert that the essential mechanism of progress is failure. Popper views the falsification of conjectures as the fulcrum that moves scientific knowledge forwards: we eliminate the bad theories, leaving the good ones to flourish. When a theory is falsified, we should be happy; we've learned something. Similarly, Darwin teaches us that the mechanism of natural selection is the elimination of weaker organisms in favour of stronger ones: the failure of one organism makes room for the success of another. Evolution would never have produced us if the earlier species, going back to protozoa, had been perfectly satisfactory, and I *suppose* this is a good thing. There is trial and error, failure and elimination, and then replacement by something that fails less. Learning a sport is like that: you start by producing certain movements in certain conditions; these movements fail, and fail again; eventually you produce movements that don't fail as much (although they will still fail sometimes). There's a process of natural selection here, as some movements are eliminated and others take their place. Alternatively, the implicit theory in your head that guides your actions is subjected to repeated falsifications, until a theory that can withstand falsification better becomes installed. The point is that failure is your friend, as it is the friend of the scientist and of the evolutionary mechanism. It's all part of the process, what makes progress possible. Failure is fine and good, really.

The thing is, we don't *like* failure. Failure doesn't feel pleasant to us. Hedonically, it stinks. But your *brain* likes failure. It thrives on failure. When your brain has been failing for a time, it finally figures out a way to fail less of the time. Meanwhile, *you* suffer, what with all that wretched failing to contend with. Your brain even has the decency and tact to work on reducing its failure rate while you're sound asleep. We are all familiar with the experience of struggling with a skill one day and finding the next day that the skill has been miraculously acquired over night. That's your brain making the most of your failures of the day before. It looks at those failures and makes the necessary adjustments, and then, hey presto! Your brain isn't pained by your failures; it relishes them. *You* are pained, but what do you matter, as long as the skill comes out right in the end? So, when you're next cursing your failures, feeling bad about them, just remember that your brain is quietly humming away with them, converting them into success. This is what we call acquiring a skill.

All achievement depends on a tolerance of failure, does it not? You achieve by persisting through failure. Failure is a mark of aspiration, of aiming high. Sport gets you accustomed to failure, so that it doesn't destroy your confidence completely. But it also gets you used to transcending failure, putting it behind you. It's a simple point: you failed, yes, but you overcame that failure, even when it seemed you never would. In fact, I'd say that if you're doing it right, failure always dogs your heels, because that means you are always aiming higher. The characteristic experience of sport, at whatever level, is a feeling of irritation at your own ineptitude. You can never feel complacent. This encourages humility and a striving to do better. The modesty of champions is often completely honest: they know full well what shots they flubbed and the things that still need to be perfected. Finitude is part of the human condition, otherwise known as "screwing up". The essence of sport is striving, failing, finally succeeding; then striving, failing again, and succeeding again – and so on in an endless cycle. But it is a healthy and instructive cycle.

Further reading

For further detailed discussion of the issue of drugs in sport, as well as other questions, see Drew A. Hyland's *Philosophy of Sport* (Minnesota: Paragon House, 1990), Sheryle Bergmann Drewe's *Why Sport?* (Toronto: Thompson Educational Publishing, 2003), and Douglas Husak's *Legalize This! The Case for Decriminalizing Drugs* (London: Verso, 2002). The other books that have come up in the course of this one include: Ludwig Wittgenstein, *Philosophical Investigations* (Oxford: Blackwell, 1958), Vladimir Nabokov, *Lolita* (New York: Vintage, 1991) and Plato, *The Republic*, Desmond Lee (trans.) (Harmondsworth: Penguin, 1987). But this is not a bookish book, so I see no reason to bloat this bibliography further.

Index